EDWIN P. HOYT served in the U.S. Army Air Corps and in the Office of War Information before he became a war correspondent for United Press International. He also worked for both the *Denver Post* and the American Broadcasting Company in the Far East, Europe, and the Middle East in the years following World War II. Hoyt is the author of many military history books, including *The Men of the Gambier Bay*, *McCampbell's Heroes*, *Bowfin*, and *The Sea Wolves*, as well as the War in the Central Pacific series: *Storm Over the Gilberts*, *To the Marianas*, and *Closing the Circle*.

Other Avon Books by
Edwin P. Hoyt

BOWFIN

CLOSING THE CIRCLE:
War in the Pacific: 1945

MCCAMPBELL'S HEROES

THE MEN OF THE GAMBIER BAY

THE SEA WOLVES:
Germany's Dreaded U-Boats of WW II

STORM OVER THE GILBERTS:
War in the Central Pacific: 1943

TO THE MARIANAS:
War in the Central Pacific: 1944

Coming Soon

LEYTE GULF:
The Death of the Princeton

THE CARRIER WAR

EDWIN P. HOYT

AVON
PUBLISHERS OF BARD, CAMELOT, DISCUS AND FLARE BOOKS

All photographs in the insert are courtesy of the National Archives.

AVON BOOKS
A division of
The Hearst Corporation
105 Madison Avenue
New York, New York 10016

Copyright © 1972 by Edwin P. Hoyt
Published by arrangement with the author
Library of Congress Catalog Card Number: 86-92087
ISBN: 0-380-75360-X

First Avon Printing: August 1987

AVON TRADEMARK REG. U.S. PAT. OFF. AND IN OTHER COUNTRIES,
MARCA REGISTRADA, HECHO EN U.S.A.

Printed in the U.S.A.

K-R 10 9 8 7 6 5 4 3 2 1

CONTENTS

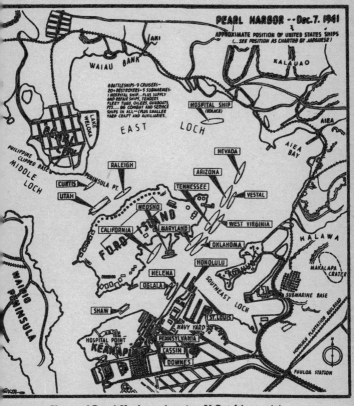

Chart of Pearl Harbor, showing U.S. ship positions

The Carrier War

At 7:55 on the morning of December 7, 1941, Rear Adm. W.R. Furlong was pacing the deck of the U.S.S. *Oglala*, tied up at a buoy in Hawaii's Pearl Harbor. He spotted a plane flying low over Ford Island, coming in from the northeast, and he watched it idly. It was a beautiful morning; the sun had come up over Mount Tantalus about an hour before, and it splashed brightly on the surface of the harbor. The blue of the water and the blue of the sky had never seemed clearer. The dawn had never seemed calmer. Even the snow-white clouds that drifted across the sky looked lazy and content.

And then all hell broke loose. The plane dropped a bomb on the seaplane ramp at the south end of the island, and a cloud of dust and debris soiled the clear air. In a moment there were more planes zooming down, dropping bombs, torpedoes, and strafing with machine guns. The Sunday morning quiet erupted into a torrent of explosions, sirens, whistles, shouts, and screams.

The Japanese were attacking Pearl Harbor.

1

CHAPTER ONE

Dawn Breaks at Pearl Harbor

Had any American naval officers been present at Kagoshima Bay on the island of Kyushu in the fall of 1941 they would have found the Japanese navy engaged in a very strange—and eerily familiar—exercise. In Kagoshima Bay Japanese naval experts had reproduced as closely as possible a Pearl Harbor in miniature. Japanese carrier pilots flew over the miniature day after day, learning to recognize the roadstead of Pearl Harbor. There was Ford Island; there was the proud Pacific Fleet with its proud battleships; there was the arsenal with its docks and drydocks; there were Hickam Field, Wheeler Field, and Kaneohe Field, all cleverly duplicated.

Of course there were no American naval officers on that part of Kyushu then; had any crept in, they most certainly would never have escaped to tell the tale—because the Japanese, under the cloak of deepest secrecy, were preparing the carrier attack on Pearl Harbor. Adm. Isoroku Yamamoto, commander-in-chief of the Japanese fleet, had been planning the attack since January. The big problem was the geography of Pearl Harbor itself. The roadstead was only 550 yards wide and 40 feet deep. The torpedo planes that would go after the big ships had a problem: how could they keep their "tin fish" from striking bottom after they were launched? Vice Adm. Chuichi Nagumo was given this problem to solve. He called in Comdr. Minoru Genda, who was planning the air phase of the attack, and Lt. Comdr. Mitsuo Fuchida, who would actually lead the attacking planes against Hawaii. They studied the problem from every angle. By November they had solved it: they would fit the torpedoes specially with ailerons, so that they could travel in a shallow dive.

The training ended in mid-November. Commander Genda had assembled 432 planes, which would go aboard six aircraft carriers. For the first time in history a naval force would go into action depending on its aircraft carriers. The whole purpose of the mission was to bring those 432 planes into action over Hawaii—and for that purpose Admiral Yamamoto had invented an entirely new strategy of war. Other nations were using their aircraft carriers to provide an "air umbrella" over a fleet of battleships. (That was the American doctrine, until men like Adm. Ernest King and Adm. William F. Halsey convinced the top admirals that carriers could be offensive weapons.) But the Japanese were going to stake everything on one swift blow with carriers. They had ten carriers in commission, compared to the seven of the United States, divided between two oceans.

The planes included 103 Nakajima torpedo bombers, which would carry sixteen-inch converted naval shells to drop on the American battleships. Another 40 Nakajimas would carry the special shallow-water torpedoes. Besides these, 131 Aichi-99 dive-bombers would dart down on the American ships, and 79 Mitsubishi fighter planes would protect the bombers against American planes. The rest of the 432 planes would be held in reserve in case a second strike was needed.

The pilots were probably then the best trained in the world. They ran races, practiced judo, and fenced with cutlasses to keep in shape. They were trained in night maneuvers so they could see with the eyes of a cat. They flew every day, practicing for their very special mission, until they had mastered every detail.

And in mid-November they were ready.

On November 19, five I-16 submarines sailed for the Hawaiian islands. These were very special submarines: inside their hulls they carried special suicide crews, and attached to their decks were midget submarines that would try to penetrate Pearl Harbor and add to the destruction.

But the big effort was to be made by the six carriers: *Kaga,* *Akagi, Soryu, Hiryu, Shokaku,* and *Zuikaku.* The first two carriers, *Kaga* and *Akagi,* were built on hulls originally designed for 40,000-ton battleships. The second pair, *Soryu* and *Hiryu,* were much smaller, at 10,000 tons. The third pair, *Shokaku* and *Zuikaku,* were the most modern in the fleet; they displaced 26,000 tons each.

These carriers were assembling far to the north at Etorofu island in the Kuriles, facing the cold Sea of Okhotsk. From the southern islands, from the Inland Sea, from all over Japan, the ships came north to this quiet hiding place and anchored in the deepwater harbor of Tankan Bay. In Tokyo Admiral Yamamoto put the finishing touches to his plan, and then radioed Vice Admiral Nagumo to put it into effect. The attack would be made at dawn, Sunday, December 7, because the Japanese knew it was the American habit to bring the fleet into Pearl Harbor every weekend so that about half the men could go ashore.

Admiral Nagumo received the message aboard the carrier flagship *Akagi.* He called his officers to a meeting and informed them of the impending attack. Preparations were speeded up. The ships were fueled. Ammunition was loaded aboard the carriers and their escorting battleships, destroyers, and cruisers. By November 22 all the necessary ships were there, and last-minute preparations were made. There was scarcely anyone to see them: the whole evidence of civilization on the shore consisted of a wireless station, a small concrete pier, and three houses where fishermen lived.

Admiral Nagumo was making careful preparations. Several thousand drums of fuel oil had been brought up to Tankan Bay, and these were now loaded aboard the carriers to be used in case it was too rough at sea to fuel from the oilers. As this work proceeded, the mechanics were working over their planes, and in the ready rooms of the carriers the pilots went to briefing sessions, where their leaders went over the instructions again and again at the blackboard.

The morning of November 26 dawned dark and foggy, and a strong wind blew through the harbor so that the ships pitched and tossed at their moorings. But not for long, for this was the day of action. At 0900 the fleet set out, nineteen warships accompanied by eight oilers and supply ships, steaming in formation, the destroyers out in front and on the sides. Orders came down from the flagship: sink any American, British, or Dutch ship seen, and board any neutral vessels and be sure they sent no radio messages.

As the destroyers moved out into the open sea, the cold spray slapped up to their bridges, and they pitched like corks in a pail of water. Even the carriers bucked in the heavy waves, and men bounced this way and that as they moved along the slippery decks. The fleet headed east, moving slowly to conserve fuel. Admiral Nagumo was very nervous, and he had reason to be. In war games played earlier that year, the attack on Pearl Harbor had brought tremendous casualties. Admiral Yamamoto had earlier advised strongly against war with the United States, but now that his government seemed bent on it, the navy was taking the only course that might bring victory: a surprise attack to knock out the American fleet and perhaps force the United States to sue for peace before it could rebuild its navy. Even now, at the last minute, the attack was still tentative. Admiral Nagumo had orders to break off and return to Japan if discovered by the Americans before December 6. Further, Admiral Nagumo knew that he might receive a message at any time telling him to come home.

But the days went by, and no message came. Nor were the ships detected; the weather was too bad for that. The signal flags run up the shrouds tore and blew to pieces almost before they could be read. Lookouts suffered from exhaustion and frostbite in the cold, heaving seas. Men were washed overboard and lost, without hope of rescue in the storm.

Admiral Nagumo waited aboard *Akagi*. For the moment the key man of the fleet was Comdr. Gishiro Migura, the flagship navigator. At this point the success or failure of the mission was dependent on his skill. He bent over his chart table with pencils and rules, his task made all the more pressing because of the weather and the infrequency with which the Japanese could see the sky.

Up and down the flag bridge the admiral paced, waiting,

waiting. He found it hard to eat, hard to concentrate. That day wore away slowly, and then the next. Then it was December 2. That night, Admiral Nagumo went to his sea cabin to get some rest. He was lying down when an officer came into the cabin and handed him a message. He read the words: *Niitaka Yama Nobure*—Climb Mount Niitaka.

Attack! That was what this coded signal meant.

All the other orders remained in force, but Admiral Nagumo could heave a sigh of relief. At least he knew now what had to be done.

The double column of carriers sailed on, moving eastward and southward toward Hawaii. Now Lieutenant Commander Ono, the fleet intelligence officer, was the key figure. He collected information, the vital data coming from the Japanese consulate in Honolulu, where a day-and-night watch was being kept on the movements of the American Pacific fleet.

On December 6, Lieutenant Commander Ono entered the admiral's cabin to report to the staff. Five of the eight battleships had returned to harbor on November 29, and two more had returned that very day. One seemed to be in drydock. Yes, the battleships were in Pearl Harbor, but not the carriers. *Enterprise* and *Lexington* were at sea in the Pacific. *Saratoga* was known to be under repair at San Diego. *Wasp* was in the Atlantic. *Langley* was with the Asiatic fleet in the Philippines. *Yorktown* and the new *Hornet* were in places unknown.

Commander Genda, the fleet operations officer, was dismayed because the carriers were nowhere to be found by the Japanese. "What a pity," he said. He had been dreaming of a clean sweep, of knocking out America's air power in the Pacific, in one swift blow.

But Admiral Kusaka, the chief of staff, was sure the carriers would remain at sea. They would have to be satisfied with the battleships, and indeed, both Kusaka and Admiral Nagumo were very well satisfied that they had caught the eight battleships in harbor all at once.

The staff meeting broke up in an atmosphere of determination. Some of the younger officers were talking bravely now, saying it was too bad they had not brought along an invasion force to take control of Hawaii. Only the senior officers knew how dangerous was the whole business on which they were embarked. And back in Tokyo Admiral Yamamoto knew best of all. He sent a message to Nagumo for the fleet: "The Empire's destiny depends on this battle," it read. "Everyone will do his duty."

When that message arrived, late in the afternoon of December 6, the Japanese battle fleet was heading south, in toward the Hawaiian islands a little more than five hundred miles away. The signal flags moved up and down the ships' superstructures as messages were sent to direct the fleet in its movement. They flapped heartily, but they no longer tore and broke away. The weather was better, and Commander Genda and the other airmen hoped anxiously for good enough conditions the next day to mount the operation.

At 2100 Admiral Nagumo presided over a strange ceremony on board *Akagi,* where all hands who were not needed on duty were summoned to the flight deck. The admiral said a few words. The commanders who would lead the flights the next day also spoke. And then a famous banner was hoisted up to the masthead of the flagship—the same flag that Admiral Togo had run up the mast of his flagship just before the Battle of Tsushima Strait in 1905, when he wiped out the Russian fleet.

There were cheers—*banzai,* may you live 10,000 years—and on the flight deck the men burst into the national anthem. Then the ship and the fleet settled down for the night—except for the lookouts and the men on watch, who guided the ships ever nearer to the enemy.

There was little sleep for the admiral. The adventure could still be called off, and might be. At five o'clock on the morning of December 7, the cruisers *Chikuma* and *Tone* each launched a seaplane to carry out last-minute reconnaissance over Pearl Harbor, to see if the American fleet actually was still in harbor. As the planes were launched, the ships pitched and rolled, but the planes got off safely. The weather was not growing any worse. They could fly.

The float planes reported back. The fleet was there, in the harbor—all except those carriers and the cruisers and destroyers that traveled with them. The battleships were lying at anchor, quiet and gray in the early predawn light.

At six o'clock Admiral Nagumo was on his bridge. The fleet had reached the launching point. The moment had come. In the carriers, the pilots and crew members were in the briefing rooms. On *Akagi,* Lieutenant Commander Fuchida stood at the blackboard and went over his objectives one more time. Then he left the room and climbed to the upper bridge, where Admiral Nagumo was waiting.

"I am ready to carry out my mission," he said.

The admiral smiled and shook his hand. "I have confidence in you," he answered. Fuchida saluted, and they both went down to the briefing room, where the admiral inspected the men who would lead the raid. The men each took a small cup of sake, Japanese rice wine, and downed it. The cheers of *banzai* went up again, and then it was time.

A few moments later admiral and air crews were on the flight deck, and Captain Hasegawa, commander of the *Akagi,* issued orders for the planes to begin taking off.

Lieutenant Commander Fuchida would fly a three-man Nakajima bomber, and he alone would have a radio transmitter in operation. He would direct the pilots of the first wave as they moved in to attack. He stepped to his plane, taking from the mechanics a red and gold *hashimaki,* or ceremonial headband of the kind the old samurai wore into battle. He wrapped it around his head and climbed into the cockpit. The engine of his plane snarled and then started up and began to roar with a growing impatience.

First went the fighters, responding to the deck control officer's green lamp—it was too dark yet to use batons. The pilots watched the officer and the lamp, and as he swung his arm around, one by one they gunned their motors and took off. On *Akagi* Admiral Nagumo's personal battle flag was raised aloft beneath that historic banner of Admiral Togo.

The scene was almost the same aboard the five other carriers. The pilots manned their planes, and the seamen cheered as they took off, fighters first, into the wind, charging down the wooden deck, almost dropping off the edge of the plunging carriers, then gaining momentum and soaring upward to circle and wait for the bombers. Finally Fuchida took off, just as the sun began to move above the horizon. He assembled the planes in formation—180 of them in this first strike—and headed for Pearl Harbor. It was not quite six thirty in the morning, and they had about an hour's flying time to reach their destination.

The carrier changed course and headed back in the direction she had come. Admiral Nagumo wanted to take no chances of discovery now that his force was committed.

Above, Fuchida began to climb. He led the big bombers, and off to his right were the torpedo planes and to his left were the dive bombers and fighter planes. The speed of the force, about 150 miles an hour, was set by the Nakajimas, for they were the slowest planes. A tail wind pushed them along this morning, so they had no fear about making their objective as far as fuel was concerned. There was a problem of navigation, or would have been if the Americans had not been so helpful. The Japanese could not calculate their drift because the clouds hid the sea from them. But Lieutenant Commander Fuchida zeroed his radio in on the American station that was transmitting. By fixing the radio beam, he could ride it right into Pearl Harbor. The Americans could hardly have made it simpler: they were delivering weather reports in the clear for the benefit of a group of B-17s that was on its way to the islands. The reporter informed Lieutenant Commander Fuchida that the weather in Hawaii was excellent, partly cloudy with a ceiling of 3500 feet, and with good visibility. What more could Fuchida ask?

The planes droned on, climbing slowly. Around 0700 Fuchida saw the lines of the coast appear through the breaking clouds, and soon the force was over Kahuku Point.

Now Lieutenant Commander Fuchida bore the responsibility for a fateful decision. If the Americans were alert, he was to fire two flares—and the dive bombers would rush in to create confusion, the high-altitude bombers would go after the guns, and the torpedo planes would sneak in low, under cover of the fighters, and go for the battleships. But if he fired one flare instead of two, that would mean they had surprised the enemy. Then the torpedo planes would go in first, the high-level bombers would move, and the dive bombers would come last concentrating on the airfields.

Fuchida fired one flare. The fighter commander, Lieutenant Commander Itaya, did not see it, and went serenely on. Fuchida rushed after, aimed his flare pistol and fired again. This time Itaya got the message, but the dive-bombers, having seen two flares, adopted the "discovery" plan, and headed in first.

Just then the scouting planes reported. There were ten battleships in the harbor, they said, plus other lighter vessels, but there were no carriers. Fuchida had been hoping, but now it was definite. The carriers were at sea.

Actually in the harbor that day were eight battleships, two heavy cruisers, six light cruisers, 29 destroyers, and many lesser ships. Seven of the battleships were moored; the eighth, *Pennsylvania*, was in drydock.

The hunting would be good. Fuchida radioed the planes about him: Attack. It was 0749.

Lieutenant Commander Takahashi, the leader of the dive-bombers, split his force, and the planes headed in, half toward Ford Island and half toward Wheeler Field. It was one of Takahashi's planes that Admiral Furlong watched that morning as it zoomed in over Ford Island and dropped its bomb.

Above, Fuchida stopped for a moment, and sent a one-word signal to Admiral Nagumo. *Tora*, said the message—tiger—and it meant that the surprise attack had begun.

Below the dive-bombers and torpedo bombers were moving in against their targets as Fuchida began the attack of the high-altitude bombers. They divided into groups of ten and headed for the targets they had studied for so long.

For minutes the Americans seemed stunned; then the guns on the ships and land began to open up. Fuchida's ship was hit almost immediately, the left rudder control damaged by an antiaircraft shell that holed the port side of the fuselage. He went on, was hit again, but still remained in the air.

The Nakajimas moved in on the battleships. They overshot, and clouds came between them and the ships, and they had to come around again. The squadron behind them began bombing, and huge red gouts of flame and spirals of smoke rose in the air.

They came from *Arizona*, which was soon a burning wreck. The smoke that poured out of her, black and oily, obscured *Nevada*, which was Fuchida's target, and he led his squadron then against *Maryland*, which seemed to be unhurt. The planes came around again, dropped their bombs, saw that two of them had hit the target, and began to move away, back toward the carriers. Fuchida led his men north for a few miles, then turned back to watch the results of his strike, for he was commander and was responsible for all of it. What he saw pleased him: *Utah* was sunk, *West Virginia* and *Oklahoma* seemed hard hit. *Arizona* was smoking and burning. *California* seemed to be sinking. Only *Pennsylvania*, over in the drydock, seemed unhurt. The airfields were littered with broken, destroyed American aircraft, and the hangars and other buildings were burning.

Lieutenant Commander Fuchida circled again and waited. He was looking for the second wave, which should have left the carriers about an hour earlier, and should be moving in. Then the job would be completed.

In the harbor, the Americans were trying to restore order from the confusion brought about by the surprise attack. They had been expecting trouble, but not like this. When torpedoes smashed into the sides of the cruiser *Raleigh* and the battleship *Utah*, the American torpedo experts could not believe it. It was well known that Pearl Harbor was too shallow for a successful torpedo attack. Then a torpedo found *Helena*. The bombs and torpedoes came thick and fast as the planes seemed to crisscross in their flights across the area. *Nevada* was one of the first ships to get her antiaircraft weapons going, and probably hit the first Japanese plane to fall, a torpedo bomber that managed to leave its calling card first, as an explosion on her port bow showed. But the price was cheap—a few minutes after the attack began, mortally wounded *Oklahoma* rolled slowly and capsized; she was a symbol of what happened to the American battleship fleet that day.

Lieutenant Commander Fuchida's first wave moved back toward the carriers they were to meet at the predetermined position, hopefully out of range of American counterattack. All this while, Admiral Nagumo was anxiously aware of the failure of the attackers to find the American carrier task forces. As a carrier man himself, the admiral knew very well what could happen to him. At this moment he was vulnerable, bound on a course to pick up his first wave of planes, his second wave away from the fleet now; his protection lay in the battleships, cruisers, and destroyers, and the thin lines of a few planes kept back for defensive patrol.

Lieutenant Commander Shimazaki led the second wave of 170 planes, which moved in over Oahu just about the time that *Oklahoma* turned turtle. Shimazaki himself led some fifty high-altitude bombers toward Hickam Field and the naval air station at Kaneohe. Their job was to wipe out aerial defenses and thus assure the safety of the fleet once it left these waters. But with the carriers of the Americans still at sea, no assurance of safety was complete.

Over Kakuku Point, Lieutenant Commander Egusa peeled off the general formation with his dive-bombers. They would go back to Pearl Harbor and mop up what was left of the American fleet.

The smoke was high in the sky now, both from burning ships and from the antiaircraft barrage that the Americans put into action once the element of surprise was wiped out. In a way, the antiaircraft fire was helpful to Lieutenant Commander Egusa: he chose as targets those ships that seemed to be putting up the heaviest fire, assuming those to be the least hurt, and went after them.

The Americans were aroused now, and their antiaircraft fire was more effective. Aided by the surprise factor, the first wave had lost only three fighters, one dive-bomber, and five torpedo planes; the second wave would lose six fighters and fourteen dive-bombers. But the Japanese pilots of the second wave knew that theirs was the more dangerous role, and they welcomed it, for the whole of this attack force had been keyed up for days to this moment.

Above Pearl Harbor the dive-bombers dropped with screaming speed, bombed, and pulled out, roaring, to climb and get away. In an hour it was all over; all the planes had dropped their bombs and torpedoes. A few moved in low over the area, machine-gunning, and then the Japanese air fleet turned away and headed north and west, as columns of smoke continued to climb high in the air above Oahu and drift out to sea.

All this while Lieutenant Commander Fuchida had circled the area, watching. He was surprised not to see any American planes in the air. (There actually were a few, but very few.) He was pleased to see that the Americans had kept their planes on the fields in tight order, so the bombing had been most effective. The airfields were littered with broken bombers and fighters. In midmorning, when it was all over, Fuchida made one last circle and then set his course north, following the second wave, like a shepherd gathering up his flock. Not far north of the islands he encountered a fighter that waggled its wings and asked for help. The fighters had taken off without any navigational safeguards, and this pilot was completely lost, without Fuchida would never have made it back to the fleet. The fighter pilot fell in behind Fuchida and tagged after him as he moved back, first to a rendezvous point where another straggler appeared, and then for anxious minutes to the carriers. The return trip was an anxious time; so many things could happen. The weather could close in, and the planes could overfly the carriers, run out of fuel, and crash into the sea—that was the most apparent and greatest danger. Or the plane could malfunction after so long in the air and begin eating up fuel or oil, running out before the point of rendezvous. Or the pilot could get lost and fly in the wrong direction. Today any of these dangers meant death, for the attack force was deep in enemy territory.

For an hour and a half they flew on, the steady drone of the engines comforting them. Fuchida looked around him, watching for enemy fighters that might pounce down. But he saw nothing save the blue of sea and the white and gray of the clouds in the sun.

Then the attack leader started and leaned forward. Ahead he could see the snaky lines of wakes across the sea and could make out the gray outlines of the fleet, the flat welcome decks of the carriers. He headed down and circled his own carrier, *Akagi*. With approving eyes he saw that the after deck was clear for his landing, that the others had returned and the planes were stacked up with wings nearly touching. He moved into the landing pattern, the plane flattened out above the deck and dropped down, tires squeaking as they punched into the wood, and the arrester wire caught the tail hook.

Still wearing his *hashimaki*, Fuchida climbed wearily from the plane, but his step was brisk as he hurried to the bridge and saluted Admiral Nagumo.

"Four battleships sunk," he said.

The admiral was pleased. "May we conclude that we have obtained the results on which we counted?" he asked.

Fuchida was careful now. He described the capsizing of one battleship, the sinking of another, and the settling down of others. He spoke of the destruction of port facilities and the planes on the fields. But he was still cautious. They had not destroyed everything by far, said the flight leader, and he would recommend a second attack.

Admiral Nagumo considered. He and his chief of staff left the bridge and went off to his cabin to confer. What were the prospects? He could assume that the Americans were now reorganizing and would be alert for any further attack; so the surprise factor was gone. And where were those American carrier task forces? He had not the slightest idea. He knew that a great deal had been accomplished in the first attack, that the American battleship fleet had been put out of action, which meant that the Americans could not move in force to Asiatic waters to fight against the Japanese expansion that was already beginning there. Signals received as the fleet waited for Fuchida indicated that the Americans had at least fifty planes left to fight with, and that was not good. Again it came back to the whereabouts of those American carriers—and submarines—now that every allied vessel would be on the lookout for the fleet.

So Admiral Nagumo gave his order, and signal flags were hoisted on the flagship. There would be no second attack. The attack force would proceed north at flank speed to escape these dangerous waters.

As Admiral Nagumo's fleet sped homeward, the Americans swung into action. Immediately a search was launched from the carriers at sea, but erroneous reports put the Japanese force off to the south of Hawaii rather than to the north, and the attack force was never discovered. It could not be discovered from the land, for the airfields had been hard hit.

The Americans knew they were at war by the end of that morning. Perhaps Lieutenant Commander Fuchida had been right; *Arizona* and *Oklahoma* were out of the war, but the other ships had different stories. *Pennsylvania* would soon be fit again. *Maryland* and *Tennessee* were sent back to the mainland and were ready for action later in the next year. *Nevada, California,* and *West Virginia* would also come back. Yet the Japanese had accomplished their aim: they had made sure that the Americans would not interfere as they moved (even as their planes attacked Pearl Harbor surface forces were moving toward the Philippines). In the next few days the Japanese attacked the Philippines and Malaya by air and by sea. Formosa-based bombers sank the British battleship *Prince of Wales* and the cruiser *Repulse* off Singapore. An attack force including the carrier *Ryujo* took the atoll of Palau in the Marianas and would soon move against Guam, and then against Wake Island, another American possession.

Admiral Nagumo's force in part participated in the attack on Wake. He headed west as fast as he could on December 7 after hitting Pearl Harbor, but on December 15 he was ordered to detach the carriers *Soryu* and *Hiryu* and supporting ships to cover the invasion of Wake Island, and the force moved to a point 200 miles northwest of the island. That invasion occurred on December 23.

There was very nearly an encounter between the carrier forces, during this invasion. Admiral Halsey and Rear Adm. Frank Jack Fletcher had been ordered to Wake to cover the reinforcement of the islands, but before they could reach the area the American carriers were called back to Pearl Harbor by a cautious commander who believed his mission was to preserve the islands and who feared a Japanese landing attempt there.

The carrier war began then, in a series of Japanese victories that stunned the western world. Suddenly the highly touted American battleship fleet was no more powerful than a mass of rubble. Suddenly the aircraft carrier had proved what the naval supporters of airpower had been contending for a long time: that the decisive weapon in a sea war in the Pacific would be the aircraft carrier.

Japan had struck the first blows, but now it was time for the Americans to get into action.

CHAPTER TWO

Halsey Strikes Back

Hardly were the clouds of smoke cleared away from the air above Pearl Harbor than there was a change of command, and Adm. Chester Nimitz came to Hawaii to prosecute the war.

Nimitz's problem was to find fighting admirals who would move against the Japanese with enough skill and daring to make up for the deficiencies in ships and planes. He began trying out his carrier admirals, for only thus could he learn which of them could fight most effectively.

On December 31, 1941, Nimitz ordered Rear Adm. Herbert F. Leary to take Task Force 14, with the carrier *Saratoga* out to the Midway area to seek out the Japanese fleet. Admiral King was very eager to have some kind of naval victory to bolster up American morale at home, because the shock of Pearl Harbor and the Japanese victories in the Philippines, Malaya, and the islands had thrown Americans into a state very near despair. There was real question in many minds as to whether the United States could win the war under any conditions. This defeatism threatened to destroy the defense effort before it had scarcely begun. And so Leary sailed.

Meanwhile, at San Diego, four transports filled with Marines moved out of port on January 6, escorted by Admiral Halsey's *Enterprise* task force. They were headed for Samoa, where the Marines would be landed to reinforce the American garrison. A few days out of port the force was joined by a new carrier task force under Rear Admiral Fletcher around the carrier *Yorktown*. With three carriers heading for enemy waters, Admiral King hoped he would stimulate some action soon.

The action came, but it was not quite what Admiral King wanted. Leary's force worked gingerly around Midway and then started home without stirring up any Japanese. Five hundred miles south of Oahu, a Japanese submarine torpedoed *Saratoga* on the night of January 11. The "fish" slammed into the port quarter, killed six men, and flooded three of the fire-rooms. *Saratoga* managed to steam back to Pearl Harbor, but she was sorely hurt and could not go out again to fight at this stage. Instead she headed for the West Coast and major repairs.

Halsey's force steamed on, but he was on a special mission and really did not want trouble until after those Marines were landed. The next American move was by Vice Adm. Wilson Brown and the *Lexington* task force. Nimitz ordered Brown to attack Wake Island. He was about 150 miles west of Oahu when the oiler *Neches* of the task force was torpedoed and sunk. That was the only oiler he had, so Brown turned around and went back to Pearl Harbor.

To this point, American carrier operations had shown a dismal lack of aggressiveness, and the admirals involved were blamed. Very shortly Leary was sent to other duty, for King and Nimitz had no time to give men a second chance in this war.

These failures did nothing to help the negative attitudes that were building in America and even within the navy. King knew this—better than anyone else—so his next move was to order Halsey to take Fletcher and strike the Japanese just as soon as those troops were unloaded.

Halsey could not have been happier. This bulldog-jawed admiral was a fighter, through and through. As a midshipman he had been a football hero, as a destroyer commander he had once launched an audacious attack against the fleet's battle-ships in war games that won for his side but also caused a million dollars worth of damage because his "tincans" rammed dummy torpedoes into the battlewagons from such short range. When he was fifty years old and decided to go into naval aviation, Halsey had taken the pilot's course, although all he had to do was qualify as an observer. He was a "lousy" pilot, but he *was* a pilot, and no one had ever heard of him backing away from a fight.

Now Bill Halsey would go out and earn the name "Bull" from press and public, and he would show King and Nimitz that he was the best fighting man they had.

The Japanese were concentrating planes and ships in the Marshall Islands, and that was to be the target area. Fletcher would go after the southern islands in *Yorktown;* Halsey would hit the northern area with the planes of *Enterprise*. He wold also send Rear Adm. Raymond A. Spruance off in the heavy cruiser *Northampton* to bombard Wotje.

On *Enterprise* Halsey was in his glory: he was going to get into action at last. What he had thought about the recall from the Wake Island relief in December was unprintable. Now, for the first time, he would lead a raid deep into the Japanese-mandated islands, far beneath the skin of the enemy empire.

So he moved. The task force steamed toward the islands at thirty knots and on the early morning of February 1, long before daylight, *Enterprise* began to launch planes in the bright moon's glow over a glassy sea. Nine torpedo planes and thirty-seven dive-bombers sped off the carrier's deck, headed for Roi and Kwajalein. Then the shuttle began, with bombers moving from one target to another, returning with encouraging stories of the planes and ships they had sunk. (Later reports indicated, however, that they did not sink any ships.)

There was plenty of action that day. For nine hours Bill Halsey maneuvered his *Enterprise* in a rectangle only five by twenty miles, an idea that would have been considered suicidal by a less aggressive commander. The Japanese shot back with planes and shore artillery. The cruiser *Chester* was attacked by eight two-engined Japanese bombers, and took one bomb that killed eight men and wounded eleven. But Halsey was lucky as well as aggressive and skillful. About 1300 he sensed that he had been in the area long enough for the Japanese defenses in the whole island chain to be alerted, and that he could expect heavy air attacks from the enemy if he continued. So "Haul ass with Halsey" became the keyword; the planes were called home to the carrier, and he began to move.

How right Halsey was. The Japanese were swarming like angry bees. Forty minutes after he moved, a "Betty," a twin-engined bomber, made a pass with its weapons and missed; then the pilot decided to sacrifice his life for the Emperor and sink a carrier. The Betty came zooming in on the flight deck of the *Enterprise*.

On the ship's bridge, the officer of the deck shouted "Hard right" to the quartermaster at the wheel, and the ship began to turn. On the flight deck, an aviation mechanic named Bruno Gaida jumped into the rear cockpit of a bomber and began firing.

On the admiral's bridge, the staff ducked, and Bill Halsey ended up on the bottom of the pile. He picked himself up, saw a sailor grinning at him, grinned back at this man who did not even seem to be afraid, and promoted him on the spot. There were two more near misses by bombers, and then *Enterprise* was safely away.

Frank Jack Fletcher's attack in the south had not been nearly as successful in any respect. Six planes of the *Yorktown* failed to come back. The Halsey group came away whistling and cheering, but somehow Fletcher never gave the men the same feeling of "doing something."

Thus Halsey's reputation was made, both with the public and with King and Nimitz. He received the Distinguished Service Medal for the attack, and the papers gave him every medal they could. For the first time someone had struck a blow back at the men who wrecked Pearl Harbor.

Halsey's boldness was cherished all the more by Americans because the news from the rest of the Pacific was so bad. The Japanese were moving steadily in the Philippines. They were crushing Southeast Asia. In the Indonesian islands the Dutch and Americans were fighting a desperate losing battle. Late in February, when the situation was critical, the old carrier *Langley* set out from Australia to ferry planes to Indonesia. On the morning of February 27, a gang of Bettys caught *Langley* as she steamed along and attacked from 15,000 feet. The captain of *Langley* turned the ship sharply to port as the bombs began to fall. The water blew up in geysers, thirty yards off the port side. The bombers came in again, and again the captain maneuvered smartly and escaped. But the Japanese were learning too, and on their third pass they strung out in a long line. The last bomber waited until *Langley* had committed herself to a turn, then swooped in and plastered the carrier with five bombs.

Langley began to list. Her planes caught fire, and the flames ran searing down the deck. She headed for the coast, her captain hoping to run in among the islands or to beach the ship and save her. Then the fire broke through bulkheads, and the engine rooms began to flood. By noon she was a raging fire on top, and the water was making way at bottom. She lost her power and slowed to a stop, dead in the water. The captain ordered the ship abandoned; survivors were picked up by a pair of destroyers, and *Langley* was sunk by torpedoes and gunfire. Thus the old carrier met an inglorious end not even fighting, but ferrying planes to battle.

This depressing news soon reached home and showed Americans that the Japanese seemed to be able to range at will in Asia and the Pacific. So Halsey, the only successful commander of these difficult days, became a kind of legendary figure in home newspapers.

Wilson Brown was to have another chance: *Lexington*'s task force was sent to the south Pacific to operate under a combined American and Australian force that was hoping to keep the Japanese from moving into an area to attack Australia. Halsey went off audaciously to attack Wake Island, and Admiral Brown headed down north of the Solomon Islands. His pilots got their glory, engaging a number of Japanese planes and shooting them down. Lt. Edward (Butch) O'Hare became an ace in one day, shooting down five Japanese planes, and the great success of the pilots against this powerful enemy raised morale everywhere, especially in the fleet. But Admiral Brown called off the attack on Rabaul that had been scheduled because the element of surprise had been lost. He was afraid to risk his carrier; there were already too few of them in the Pacific. Perhaps he was right, but Admiral King wanted more men like Halsey, who at about this time moved boldly into position to attack Marcus Island, 1,000 miles southeast of Tokyo, or, as the newspapers said, "right in

Tojo's backyard." In all this, the Japanese carriers were missing—they were being used in the fight against the Dutch in Indonesia and to drive the British away from Southeast Asia. *Akagi, Kaga, Soryu,* and *Hiryu,* under Admiral Nagumo, were very busy in the invasion of Java, and later Nagumo led an even stronger force into the Indian Ocean to attack the British naval bases in Ceylon and harass British shipping. *Akagi* was his flagship again, and this time he had the carriers *Zuikaku* and *Shokaku* along as well as *Soryu* and *Hiryu.*

The Japanese carriers had good reason for good morale, and Admiral Nagumo deserved to be proud of them and of himself. By spring he had sunk five battleships, one carrier (the British *Hermes,* sunk off Trincomalee, Ceylon), and thousands of tons of lesser ships, without losing a single vessel of his own.

But there were signs. . . .

For one thing, the Americans were learning some lessons in carrier technique. Wilson Brown came back from his raids and recommended that carriers be used at least in twos (something the Japanese knew well). So his *Lexington* and Fletcher's *Yorktown* went out raiding again in March. They attacked the Japanese in New Guinea at Lae and Salamaua; 104 planes went out, and all but one of them came home. They sank three ships, and came home cheering. But by this time, Admiral Brown was nervous about the Japanese land-based air-power at Rabaul, so near him, and the carriers sped away.

At home, morale was rising. President Roosevelt said of Wilson Brown's foray against New Guinea, "It was by all means the best day's work we have had." This statement was itself an indication of how bad things really were that spring of 1942, when almost all the other news was negative. The fact was that Japan had the men and the machines and was on the march, still carrying on the momentum of the surprise attack of 1941. Only the aircraft carriers with their hit-and-run capability were in any position to make spectacular moves against the Japanese.

So now, in the spring of 1942, Admiral King and Gen. Henry Harley Arnold of the Army Air Corps planned a really spectacular stunt that was calculated to hit where it would hurt, and give morale its biggest boost of all. They would bomb Tokyo!

The only way it could be done was by carrier. America did not have any bombers capable of traversing the huge distances involved. But the carrier could not be left to stand in on the Japanese front porch, where it would undoubtedly be sunk. The solution was to use medium-range army bombers flown off from a carrier; the carrier would then move out of danger, and after the mission the planes would land somewhere well away from Japan.

When Arnold and King began talking about the idea, and then took it to President Roosevelt, there was some hope that the planes might land in Siberia. But the Russians were not at war with Japan, and so desperate was their struggle with the Germans that they did not wish to create any situation that might give them another front to defend. The Siberia idea was canceled. The planes would have to land in China. They would be B-25 medium bombers equipped with special long-range gasoline tanks.

One afternoon early in March, Bill Halsey walked into Admiral Nimitz's office on the second deck of the headquarters building at Pearl Harbor. He was just back from the Marcus raid, but he was waiting eagerly to go out again and fight the Japanese.

Nimitz and a captain from Washington were talking. The captain was Donald W. Duncan, air officer on Admiral King's staff, and Duncan was laying out the plan that had been prepared in Washington for the army-navy operation against Japan. Halsey moved in and bent over the maps of the Pacific and the Far East. The problem was to get close enough to Japan to launch those bombers, but not so close that the Japanese could come bearing down with all their might. The trouble might be that the Japanese would use carriers and the string of islands around their empire as bases, and knock out the American task force. Halsey's job was to prevent that and get the mission into the air.

"Can you do it?" Nimitz asked.

"They'll need a lot of luck," said Halsey.

"Are you willing to take them?"

Of course Halsey was willing. He was willing to go anywhere and do anything that would strike a blow at the enemy. But there were problems. First of these was the opposition of members of the Nimitz staff to the raid. Adm. Milo Draemel, the chief of staff, felt that it was a waste of good airplanes that could be better used elsewhere. The planes would do little damage, he said, and most of them would be lost. Nimitz agreed with all that Draemel said, but ignored the final advice, because he knew better, as did King and Halsey—that the morale factor of this Tokyo raid was the important thing.

So Halsey took on a task from which he might never return.

He flew to the West Coast to talk to Lt. Col. James H. Doolittle, who would lead the raid. Jimmy Doolittle was a famous stunt and test pilot of the 1920s and 1930s, who had come back to the Air Corps as a member of Hap Arnold's staff, but who had managed to grab on to the Tokyo mission and hold it for himself. There was nothing in the world he wanted to do so much right then as lead that bombardment flight against the Japanese.

Halsey met Doolittle in a San Francisco restaurant, and they talked over the special problems of the combined raid. The most serious problem was the matter of distance from Japan. Halsey would take them in as close as he could, but if they were surprised by the Japanese, then he would have to cut and run. He could not risk the whole task force—there simply were not enough carriers available. So the decision would be made at sea, whether to take off or to push the planes into the ocean and come back without bombing. That last, desperate idea shocked Doolittle until Halsey explained: with the flight deck full of bombers, the carrier could not launch her own planes and would be a sitting duck for enemy air power. So if danger came, the bombers would have to go one way or the other, into the air or over the side.

The task force would consist of Halsey's *Enterprise,* and the new carrier *Hornet,* which would actually carry the bombers. Capt. Marc Mitscher in *Hornet* would come through the Panama Canal from Norfolk, load the planes at San Francisco Bay, then head out into the Pacific, where Halsey would meet him at a specified point. Protected by cruisers and destroyers, the task force would then move in against Japan. All these details were worked out by Captain Duncan with Captain Mitscher when *Hornet* pulled into San Diego in March. Then *Hornet* sailed for Alameda Naval Air Station, and on April 1 the sixteen B-25s that could be carried on the deck of the carrier were loaded by crane.

All this activity could not help but arouse attention in the navy yard, and army and navy intelligence devised a cover story that was supposed to fool the Japanese. It was assumed —it must be assumed—that the enemy had agents in the area, and that they would funnel their information back to Japan, perhaps through South America. So the story concocted was that *Hornet* was ferrying this load of B-25s to Hawaii, where they would be used for coastal defense.

Jimmy Doolittle went aboard the carrier. He marched down to Captain Mitscher's office, past the Marine guard at the door. The two men began planning.

The success of her cover story was tested that day in an interesting way. Just as suspected, the word had gotten around San Francisco that *Hornet*'s decks were filled with army bombers. A representative of one of the aircraft companies, along with hundreds of others, heard that *Hornet* was going to Hawaii. He came thundering down to the dock and insisted on a ride to Honolulu, where he had important business, very important business that made it imperative that he get there almost immediately. *Hornet*'s officers tried gently to dissuade him, but the aircraft man was not listening. It was not a question of hitching a free ride; since the war the military had priority on all flying to the islands, and passenger ships were not moving anywhere. It was a question of transportation. The aircraft company man stuck out his chin and threatened to go to Washington if they did not let him aboard, and everyone knew what that meant.

So reluctantly they let the airplane man come aboard for the ride. Captain Mitscher knew that the poor fellow was going to be a good long time in virtual prison. There was nothing else to be done; turning him down would have wrecked the cover story.

So the airplane man and all the others were herded aboard *Hornet* on that afternoon of April 1, and she moved out into San Francisco Bay and anchored in full view of the city. That night, bar-goers at the Top of the Mark could look out over the bay and see *Hornet* sitting there, with her cargo of airplanes outward bound.

On April 2, the *Hornet* headed out, now part of Task Group 16.2, which consisted of the cruiser *Vincennes*, the light cruiser *Nashville*, the oiler *Cimarron*, and four destroyers. They moved through the Golden Gate Bridge and out to sea. That afternoon, Captain Mitscher got on the loudspeaker system and told the men of the ship what many of them suspected anyhow, and what the airplane manufacturer's man now learned to his dismay: they were not going to Hawaii, they were going to Japan, to within 400 miles of Tokyo if possible, to launch those sixteen B-25s "as a surprise for Premier Tojo."

The cheers rose up and echoed through the ship. What could the airplane man say? The army men and the navy men clapped each other on the backs and sang and shouted, and made up a victory song to the tune of the Seven Dwarfs' marching song from *Snow White*.

In a few hours, however, it was down to hard work. The weather socked in and *Hornet* plowed the sea, her flight deck drenched in rain and spray. The army mechanics worked over their B-25s, doing everything possible to be sure they would fly well and fast, and use as little fuel as possible.

There were miracles this trip, as there had to be if the mission was to be successful. On the oiler *Cimarron*, a man was washed overboard, as men had been washed over aboard the Japanese ships on their way through these stormy Pacific seas a few months earlier. But wonder of wonders, *Cimarron's* S1c. P.D. Williams was picked up and rescued by the destroyer *Meredith*, hauled like a little cork out of the heaving sea.

As the days went on, Jimmy Doolittle assembled his flight leaders and his pilots and briefed them exhaustively on what to expect when they took off from the carrier. They had practiced simulated carrier take-offs hour after hour, and they knew they could do that part. They had never tried a carrier landing—that was out of the question. By the time the Doolittle Raiders bombed Tokyo, the task force would be long gone, heading for other waters where the superior might of the Japanese navy could not find the Americans. These meetings were held in Captain Mitscher's cabin and offices; Mitscher had moved to his sea cabin on the bridge so Jimmy might have a place to work.

Jimmy and Mitscher met and talked from time to time, a pair of veteran airmen: the bandy-legged, smiling Doolittle, and the wizened, skinny Mitscher with his wrinkled turkey neck. They knew better than any others—except Halsey, who was moving to meet them—what their ships and planes were in for.

The army airmen studied their targets: Tokyo, Yokohama, Nagoya, Osaka—the big cities of Japan. They were coached by the carrier's intelligence officer, Lt. Stephen Jurika, who had once served in the naval attaché's office in Japan. They studied maps and photos and charts of the areas they would bomb, and tried to learn recognition points.

The airmen talked about various plans for attack. A night take-off, three hours before dawn, would be best for the bombing; they would thus catch the Japanese early in the morning, and then reach the China bases before dark. But Mitscher and Halsey would not let them light up the carriers, and the army pilots would find it hard to work in the dark. If they launched at dawn, the Japanese antiaircraft fire would have a good go at them. They might launch at dusk, bomb at night, and then reach China in the daytime.

All this was to happen on April 19, the plan said. So they planned, and the men played poker and shot craps, and hundreds and even thousands of dollars changed hands. Winning or losing did not seem to make much difference when they all knew they were heading into the jaws of the Japanese tiger. One man won $1,100 and thought nothing of it.

As *Hornet* steamed along on the morning of April 8, Admiral Halsey and *Enterprise* were moving out of Pearl Harbor with two cruisers, three more destroyers and a pair of oilers, and set course to meet *Hornet*'s half of the task force at the rendezvous in the middle of the ocean.

Halsey put out his air patrols, and every moment that the planes could fly these eyes of the fleet were out ahead, searching to be sure the task force was not spooked by the Japanese. The success of the mission depended on secrecy.

On April 16 a shock came: an announcement by Radio Tokyo that some fools were claiming they had bombed the Japanese capital. "They know it is absolutely impossible for enemy bombers to get within 500 miles of Tokyo," sneered the Japanese broadcaster. It was not a comforting thought to a task force that was moving closer to Japan every moment.

The task groups met in silence after one day's delay in the rendezvous because of the foul weather. Halsey had ordered radio silence all the way because the Japanese could monitor American radio broadcasts, take a fix on them, and discover their point of origin. A carrier force moving across the Pacific with its radio blaring was like a cart moving along a road, dropping grain from a broken bag—it would leave a trail that could be followed right to its source. So messages were carried by blinker and by semaphore as the big task force steamed along toward Japan.

On April 16, the planes were spotted on *Hornet*'s deck for take-off. Doolittle would go first, with 467 feet of clear deck ahead of him. He had a particular problem: while the other pilots had been practicing simulated carrier take-offs, he had been busy working out the details of the raid, so he had less experience in this piloting than any of his men. He would have to draw on his vast knowledge of airplanes that went back to the days of World War I when he had been a fighter pilot and an instructor. While he examined the flight deck and spoke to the men who were manicuring the bombers, the armament crews were working, bringing the bombs to the ready. In bomb storage, the fliers and the navy boys were chalking messages to the Japanese on the bombs, and Captain Mitscher turned over some Japanese medals he had been given earlier to be attached to bombs.

* * *

Next day, when they refueled at sea, the weather seemed even worse than it had been at the beginning of the trip. Huge waves bounced the tankers up and down alongside the carriers—such waves had once ripped a fueling fixture right off *Lexington*'s deck. In midafternoon the task force speeded up for the run in to the Japanese perimeter, and the weather was so bad the landing signal officer who was directing the scouting planes was rolled off his platform and finally had to get a seaman to hold him in place so he could work.

On the night of April 17, Halsey passed the word to Lieutenant Colonel Doolittle that they were moving in fast; the carrier force would run all night and the next day until they got to their point or were intercepted. So as the wind whistled overhead, the men of the carriers and their escorting ships settled down for the night.

The radar men on *Enterprise* were busy and watchful that night, for they knew they had entered the zone of intense danger. At 0310 it happened: they spotted two blips on the surface, and knew that they could be nothing but Japanese ships. The message went to the bridge, and the lookouts reported two white lights. The officer of the watch changed course, and the task force turned 90 degrees to starboard to get away from the ships. At the same time the bells began clanging to send the men to general quarters throughout the little fleet.

The watch continued. The radar men peered at their sets, and saw the blips moving along unconcernedly. They had escaped exposure, so far. For an hour they ran at right angles to their course, but then at 0415 turned back to the base course and steamed ahead for Japan.

The dawn came, an oily gray dawn, with the wind zipping along the flight decks and the rain sending spray high against the ships. The morning patrol set out from *Enterprise*, circling out to watch for the enemy. Suddenly one of the pilots looked down and spotted a patrol craft. He saw it change course and saw the men aboard pointing. He had been seen. He sped back to the carrier and dropped a message on the deck.

At the same time, another patrol vessel sighted the carriers, and began to send a radio message. The ships were only about eight miles apart; knowing that the jig was up, Halsey ordered *Nashville* to sink the patrol boat, and she tried. But the weather was so bad it was like shooting at a pinhead, and it took 925 shells to sink the little vessel. Worse, it took twenty-nine minutes, and all that time the patrol craft was sending messages to Tokyo, reporting the position of the task force.

The intelligence officers of the *Enterprise* reported that they were very badly exposed indeed—during those 29 minutes the Japanese had given Tokoyo a very good idea of their position, the constitution of the force, and had repeated it several times. They were, Halsey calculated, 650 miles from Tokyo.

It was much further out than Doolittle had hoped to be, but it was not so far out that Halsey could order Doolittle to dump the planes over the side. Halsey decided to go ahead, to take the calculated risk of running in further while they launched the planes, and then to haul out of there, fast.

Aboard *Hornet*, Jimmy Doolittle stood on the bridge with Captain Mitscher and made his calculations. It would be a dangerous raid now, more dangerous than he liked, because they would be bombing in broad daylight and landing in China at night. But there was no option—they must go now.

The ship swung into action. In the messrooms, the stewards ladled out scrambled eggs and pancakes for those not too excited to eat. On the flight deck the mechanics and air crews went over the planes one last time. Jimmy made his calculations and got ready, and at 0800 came the blinker signal from Halsey: "Launch planes. To Colonel Doolittle and his gallant command, good luck and God bless you."

The moment had come.

The army pilots went down to their planes and fussed with them those last minutes. Doolittle walked to his own plane, the first to become airborne. The preflight check of equipment and instruments began. Captain Mitscher maneuvered the carrier to bring it into the wind for the launching. They were making twenty-two knots, and with the winds coming across the bow, the propellers of the B-25s began to windmill.

On the port side of the bow stood a navy flight officer, checkered flag in hand. His motions would guide Doolittle and his boys as they moved off the carrier. Doolittle was first. He gunned the engines as much as they would take; then, when the waves were right and the officer zipped down the flag, Jimmy's plane began to lumber forward, and then gain speed. It took off just as calculated and zoomed ahead, as the *Hornet* reached the crest of a wave. A dangerous dip, and then the plane was airborne and flying on her own. Doolittle climbed and circled as he waited for his other planes to take off.

They went, one after the other. Lt. Travis Hoover was second, and here was a miscalculation. The B-25 sank at the end of the deck, and seemed sure to go into the water—but just above the waves it pulled up and moved ahead and into the safety of the air.

Plane 3 got off safely.

So did plane 4.

Plane 5 surged forward and was aloft.

So did plane 6.

Pilot Ted Lawson in plane 7 forgot to put down his flaps—which increased the air resistance and gave him more lift—and very nearly plummeted into the sea.

Planes went off smoothly, 8, 9, 10, 11, 12 13, 14, 15, . . .

Lieutenant Bill Farrow was in the last B-25. As he was ready to move to the take-off line, the sea made the carrier lurch, and the bomber began to slide backward. Crewmen and seamen rushed forward and lashed lines to the nose, but the lines snapped. Men grabbed the plane and held her down in the bucking sea. Machinist's mate Robert W. Wall backed into a propeller and lost an arm. Fellow sailors rushed to help him and get him down to sick bay for medical treatment.

Farrow moved the plane back again to the line. Air crewman Jacob De Shazer looked out and saw that the plastic nose had been damaged—there was a hole in' the nose a foot in diameter. But it was too late, the flight officer was beckoning with his checkered flag, and it was now or never. Farrow gunned the engines, and the sixteenth plane took off from

Hornet and began to climb. It was a perfect launch. They had achieved another miracle.

In ones and twos the Doolittle Raiders headed for their targets, and shortly after noon began to arrive, straggling in, from so many directions that they quite confounded the Japanese air defense. The Japanese believed that no American bombers could touch them, and so Doolittle was able to skim the treetops, so close as to see the expressions on people's faces, and he realized that most of them believed the bombers were Japanese.

Jimmy Doolittle bombed Tokyo just after noon that day, dropping fire bombs that started serious fires in various places in the city, and his boys dropped explosives on the city and on other areas too. Soon they were rocketing across the coastline, heading for the open sea, and when they were out of sight of land they changed course for China. They had achieved another miracle: all the sixteen planes had dropped their bombs, and not one of them had been shot down in the process. So far, they had made it two-thirds of the way.

But luck deserted Jimmy Doolittle's boys—at least in part —when they hit the China coast. They came in late at night, in the dark and nearly out of gas. All sixteen planes either ditched in the sea, on the coast, or the crews bailed out. Every plane was lost. More tragic, men were lost. Jimmy and his crew came through safely, but Ted Lawson, the pilot of No. 7, lost a leg. Dean Hallmark, pilot of No. 6, was captured with his crew. So was tailender Farrow. The Japanese held mock trials and finally executed Hallmark, Farrow, and Sgt. Harold Spatz of Farrow's crew. Five other Americans were held in prison, and Lt. Robert Meder died of starvation there. That was the end of the Tokyo Raid—which had accomplished everything General Arnold and Admiral King had hoped. When the announcement was made by President Roosevelt that American planes from "Shangri-La" had bombed Tokyo, the American people rose up in joy. They had their first feeling of real victory, their first sense that the war was going to be won.

When the news was released, *Hornet* and *Enterprise* were on their way back to Pearl Harbor. They had turned around as soon as the planes were launched, for they knew the Japanese would be looking for them. Suddenly, in the afternoon, Radio Tokyo announced excitedly that Tokyo was under aerial attack. There were cheers, but there was little time for them, because the task force was still in great danger. A scout plane from *Enterprise* spotted a Japanese patrol plane—but the enemy did not see the task force. Lookouts on *Hornet* spied two Japanese patrol vessels. Bombers set off and, with the help of *Nashville*'s guns, sank them. Then the task force was free, and headed home.

The word came finally to Halsey that men had been captured, and men had been killed, and then he learned of the sentencing of the fliers to death as war criminals. Halsey clenched his fist that day and spoke between his teeth.

"They'll pay," he said. "We'll make them pay."

And that became the watchword of the Bull of the Pacific. From then onward, with redoubled efforts, he set out to "Kill Japs; kill Japs, and kill more Japs."

CHAPTER THREE

The Battle of the Coral Sea

The Japanese were still moving south in the spring of 1942, and Admiral King grimly told his subordinates that they had to be stopped. If they took Australia, which seemed likely, the war might be prolonged indefinitely, or even lost. The enemy simply could not be allowed to continue to forge ahead, no matter what it cost.

The line of defense was still the carrier force. The battleships, under repair, were too slow to compete with the fast Japanese forces. The Japanese control of so many islands gave them a formidable weapon in land-based air power, too. So the carriers were all-important.

Rear Adm. Aubrey Fitch had recently been assigned to command Task Group 17.5, which was *Lexington* and her cohort of ships. Rear Adm. Frank Jack Fletcher was still in command of the *Yorktown* group. They were ordered to go into action in the South Pacific and stop the Japanese advance if they could. And on May 1, 1942, the two carrier groups linked up and began to operate as a hunter force. The object was a projected Japanese invasion of the Solomon Islands, another step on the route to Australia; the American orders were to stop them.

The Japanese moved fast. On the morning of May 3, Rear Adm. Kiyohide Shima's invasion force landed on the beaches of the island of Tulagi in the Solomons, and Admiral Fletcher, who was fueling his force, decided to attack as soon as he could. Admiral Fitch's *Lexington* had already fueled and traveled south, so Fletcher's *Yorktown* would have to work alone.

The morning of May 4 dawned stormy and cold, which was useful for Fletcher because he could hide his ships in the storm front almost until ready to strike. Only the planes would be the giveaway as they flew through clear skies. At 0630, which was before sunrise this day, the planes began taking off. First the *Yorktown* launched twelve TBD torpedo planes, then twenty-eight SBD dive bombers, and finally six F4F fighters. The bombers would proceed against the enemy, the fighters would patrol overhead.

Lt. Comdr. W. O. Burch's dive-bombers circled and headed for Tulagi, where the sky was clear. Down below they saw ships of the Japanese invasion force, and they plummeted down to drop their thousand-pound bombs. One dive-bomber zeroed in on the destroyer *Kikuzuki* and hit her so hard the Japanese had to beach her. They also sank two minesweepers.

Five minutes went by. Then Lt. Comdr. Joe Taylor's torpedo bombers swooped along the water, launching torpedoes. They sank the third minesweeper.

The American pilots were elated at what they had done. They sped back to the *Yorktown*, and landed, and took off again as soon as their planes were fueled and given new arms for the attack. An hour later they were in the air again and back over the beach, where they knocked out two seaplanes and damaged one patrol boat. That was all for the moment, but when they came back—having lost one torpedo bomber to antiaircraft fire—the pilots reported three more seaplanes anchored not far away, and Frank Jack Fletcher sent a handful of fighters after them. They strafed, zooming in low, and destroyed the seaplanes, then spotted a destroyer and made four runs on her. They did not know it, but they killed the captain and many crewmen. The fighters paid the price, though: on the trip home two F4Fs got lost and crash-landed on the south coast of Guadalcanal. Luckily there were no Japanese about, and that night the destroyer *Hammann* came in close offshore and rescued the two pilots.

The Japanese had been completely surprised at Tulagi— because an American carrier had appeared where no American carrier had a right to be.

* * *

In fact, Admiral Yamamoto, the commander-in-chief of the Japanese navy, was looking for a big battle with the Americans. He realized that as long as the American carriers existed, any Japanese invasion would be imperiled, and he had hoped with this Tulagi invasion to draw out the remains of the American fleet and crush it. The Tulagi invasion was not much—it required only a few cruisers, a seaplane tender, and the light aircraft carrier *Shoho* in support—but hoping that the Americans would emerge for battle, Yamamoto also sent down a carrier striking force under Vice Adm. Takeo Takagi, which included the big carriers *Shokaku* and *Zuikaku*. They proposed to polish off whatever the Americans and Australians had working at sea down here. There would have been more carriers, except that even as Tulagi began, Yamamoto was planning an invasion of Midway, an invasion of the Aleutians, and the big battle to completely decimate the American fleet. Here in the South Pacific he expected to find only the carrier *Saratoga*. Actually *Saratoga* was at Puget Sound naval yard in Washington, being repaired after the torpedo that had caught her in January. Japanese naval intelligence was not very accurate.

On the afternoon of May 3, Admiral Takagi's carrier force was refueling at a leisurely pace. The refueling continued on May 4. But late that day an excited staff officer appeared on the admiral's bridge with a message: Tulagi had been attacked by carrier planes. The admiral, who had been idly watching the pumps and hoses at work, straightened immediately. He went into the chart room, began making calculations, and then issued orders. The refueling was stopped, the Japanese ships made ready, and the force headed out for a point north of Santa Isabel Island in the Solomons, even as Admiral Fletcher moved south of the Solomons to join Admiral Fitch.

On the morning of May 5 patrol planes from *Yorktown* encountered a four-engine Japanese flying boat from Rabaul and shot it down. The missing plane was reported to Japanese headquarters, but no one knew where it had gone down since it had not been able to use its radio. So the Japanese began to grow edgy. But for that matter, so did Admiral Fletcher, who expected a Japanese carrier force to come down from the Rabaul area to the north. Yet May 5 was quiet, the forces were far away from one another, and there was talk on the American carriers of leave in Australia, where they would whoop it up.

On the afternoon of May 6, the Americans had a good idea of the Japanese plans. Throughout this area the Australians had coast watchers, so by this time Fletcher knew that there were three Japanese carriers at large, and that an invasion force was moving against Port Moresby. On the evening of May 6, Fletcher began moving the American carrier force north to strike at Port Moresby and the invasion attempt on the next day. He still did not know where Takagi was with his carriers, but that was made equal: Takagi did not know where he was either. At one point they were only seventy miles apart.

The Japanese found the Americans first. On the morning of May 7, Admiral Takagi ordered a plane sweep to be sure the Americans were not sneaking up on him. At 0736 one of the Japanese search planes spotted two wakes below him, moved down, and identified a carrier and a cruiser. He radioed excitedly back to the flagship, and in a few minutes a Japanese air strike was launched from *Shokaku* and *Zuikaku*. The patrol plane dropped one bomb, which missed but alerted the Americans to danger.

Unfortunately there was little that could be done; the ships in jeopardy were the oiler *Neosho* and the destroyer *Sims*. An hour and a half later, fifteen Japanese bombers came in at high level, and missed with all bombs. Then came ten more, which also missed. But finally thirty-six Japanese dive-bombers attacked *Sims*. She was hit by three 500-pound bombs, two of which exploded in the engine room. *Sims* buckled at the middle and went down stern first. Then the Japanese went after *Neosho*. They put seven direct hits into her, including one by a frustrated pilot who missed with his bomb and crashed into the ship's side, sending burning gasoline all along the deck. Eight bombs missed so nearly as to cause other damage, and men began jumping over the side, taking life rafts with them.

But *Neosho* did not sink the way *Sims* had; she floated for four days; then rescue came, the survivors were picked up off the hulk, and poor *Neosho* was scuttled.

After striking *Sims* and *Neosho,* the planes from the two big Japanese carriers headed back to their ships, and halfway home they saw *Yorktown* and *Lexington* down below them. But they had no bombs or ammunition left, and all they could do was radio the position of the American ships and rush home to rearm.

Yorktown's planes were in the air too, and they found Japanese ships. Making the same mistake Takagi's men had made, they identified the ships as carriers, when they were actually cruisers. But around 1100 on May 7, Lt. Comdr. W. L. Hamilton of *Lexington* looked down as he scouted for the enemy and found a carrier surrounded by cruisers and destroyers. It was the light carrier *Shoho*.

Lexington's planes moved in to attack. Several Zero fighters came up to meet them but were driven off. This first wave of Americans did not do much; they scored a near miss on *Shoho* which blew five planes over the side of the flight deck, but that was all. But the word was out, and the American planes from two carriers converged on the *Shoho* within minutes. In came a *Lexington* torpedo squadron, then *Yorktown* dive-bombers, then more torpedo planes from the American carriers, and more dive-bombers. Ninety-three planes were swarming around the Japanese carrier, looking for places to sting, and they found them.

A bomb smashed aft and broke the rudder controls of *Shoho* so she could not steer or evade. In a few minutes she was hit by thirteen bombs and seven torpedoes, and was burning from stem to stern. She sank at 1136, so devastated that although Japanese destroyers came alongside to fish the survivors out of the water, they found only 700 of the 1,200 men who had been aboard.

The American pilots were ecstatic. Here was the first real naval victory of the war.

"Scratch one flattop," shouted Lt. Comdr. R.E. Dixon of the *Lexington* as he made his way back to the carrier.

Now there were two Japanese carriers in the area, and the

odds seemed more even. The Americans continued to patrol, but they did not find the big carriers.

Late that afternoon of May 7, Admiral Takagi ordered *Shokaku* to send out a force of bombers and torpedo bombers to attack the American carriers. The weather had closed in, and the Japanese planes did not find the American carriers, but they were now in danger; they were running low on fuel, and the great weight of their bombs and torpedoes hampered them. So they dropped their weapons and then headed for home.

In the thickening gloom they saw carriers and moved into the pattern to begin landing—only then discovering that the carriers they wanted to land on were American carriers. They sped over at masthead height, only to encounter fighters from *Yorktown* and *Lexington*. In the air battle that followed the Americans shot down nine Japanese planes, losing two American fighters. Lt. (jg.) Paul Baker shot down three Japanese planes that day before colliding with a Zero and crashing into the sea.

The Japanese had yet more trouble: on returning to *Shokaku* in the darkness, Sublieutenant Ishikawa's dive-bomber crash-landed and tied up the flight deck for precious minutes; consequently eleven planes were destroyed in crash landings and handling that night.

Once the last of the doomed flight was in, Admiral Takagi was urged by his flight officers to stage a night attack on the American carriers, but recent experience made him hesitate. He did give the order, but then came another order from higher headquarters that made it impossible. The sinking of *Shoho* had left the Port Moresby invasion force without air cover. Takagi was to provide that cover now, said his superiors. So he withdrew the order for the night attack on *Lexington* and *Yorktown*.

On the morning of May 8, the Japanese had a search mission in the air an hour before dawn, and as the sun rose an attack force of ninety planes took off to search for the American carriers. The searchers found the Americans, and met the attack planes, and guided them to the target. At the same time, a search from *Lexington* was in the air, looking for the Japanese carriers, and Lt. (jg.) J. G. Smith found them. *Yorktown* and *Lexington* launched their air strikes. This would be a battle of carrier planes against carriers on both sides.

Yorktown's planes took off at 0915 and flew for an hour and three quarters until they found the Japanese carriers. There, 17,000 feet below, they caught a glimpse of *Zuikaku* as she headed into the protection of a rain squall; but they had more than a glimpse of *Shokaku*, which was turning into the wind, launching an air patrol.

Lt. Comdr. Joe Taylor led the attack of his Torpedo Squadron 5 against *Shokaku;* but the torpedoes were badly aimed and launched too far away from the target, and they all missed. The dive-bombers did better, scoring several hits on the carrier, and setting the flight deck afire; soon it was damaged so badly the ship could no longer launch planes, although she could recover them. The fire-fighters were at work a few minutes later when part of *Lexington*'s planes found the carrier and added one more bomb hit to the damage. But that was all. *Shokaku* was in no danger of sinking.

The Americans headed home, wrongly thinking they had seen the carrier settling. As they flew back, they could hear the sounds of the battle of their own carriers over the radio, and it was a much fiercer struggle.

At this point in the war, the Japanese pilots were better trained, better directed, and some said they had better equipment than the Americans. Certainly the Japanese were making the best of what they had this day. These two carriers were veterans of the Pearl Harbor attack, and so were their airmen. Some of them had been in action almost steadily since Pearl Harbor, ranging from Hawaii to the Indian Ocean. Now their experience was to tell.

The Japanese pilots found the Americans at almost the same time that the American pilots had found their carriers. It was the same story, almost empty carrier decks, launching a few combat air patrol planes. But the weather was fine and clear here, and the Japanese had no problem with visibility. They had altitude, and they shot down or drove off the American fighters that moved in against them.

* * *

At 1118 the Japanese came in, sun at their backs, which made them a hard target for the antiaircraft gunners on the carriers. Two groups of torpedo planes came in on *Lexington*, one from each side to keep her from escaping by maneuvering. The Americans began scoring—a torpedo bomber exploded and on the *Lexington* the men could see the parts of bodies flying through the air. But there were too many planes, too many torpedoes, and Capt. Ted Sherman could not evade them all, no matter how he turned. Two minutes after the attack began, a torpedo struck forward on the side, and then another hit just opposite the bridge. The dive-bombers came in and dropped: one bomb struck in an ammunition box and created a display of deadly fireworks; another hit the smokestack. Near misses sent up splashes and started clanging noises throughout the ship.

Over on *Yorktown* it was not as bad. The torpedo bombers came in only on the port side, and she managed to turn and avoid them.

The dive-bombers were luckier, or more skillful. One dive-bomber made a hit with an 800-pound bomb that penetrated the flight deck to the fourth deck, where it exploded, and in these confined quarters killed sixty-six men.

In nineteen minutes the attack was ended. The Japanese had expended their weapons and were heading home, even as the American planes which had hit *Shokaku* came back the other way.

The Japanese were exultant with victory. Some of *Shokaku*'s planes landed on *Zuikaku*, which could accommodate them because that carrier had lost forty-three planes in the attack. The pilots reported to the admiral that they had sunk both American carriers, and from the decks of the ships went up the cries of *banzai*—and once again the Japanese believed they were destined to know nothing but victory.

Yet Admiral Takagi knew better. He ordered the *Shokaku* to head back for Japan. She had a narrow escape on the voyage, damaged as she was; she very nearly capsized, but arrived safely in port for repairs.

Yorktown soon had her fires out and was conducting normal operations, but aboard *Lexington* it was a different story. The end of the air battle found her listing, with water in three boiler rooms and several fires burning in the ship. It did not seem bad—she was able to handle her aircraft, both launching and recovering—but the fires persisted, even though they were small and the damage control officer was sure they would be under control any moment.

They never did get under control. One small fire burned on. And then came the real damage. Someone in the heat of action had left a motor generator running on a lower deck. Gasoline vapors from a ruptured tank concentrated here, and at 1247 there was a tremendous explosion and then a whole series of explosions that knocked out the ship's communications system.

Even then there was hope. The *Lexington*'s plane operations continued without a hitch. Only those who ran the ship knew how great the damage was. There were more explosions again at 1445, and half an hour later Capt. F. C. Sherman abandoned flight operations as too dangerous under the conditions.

Destroyers and other ships came alongside to run hoses and fight the fires. Smoke poured out of the lower decks and came up along the flight deck. The fire was out of control, and the explosions indicated that it would not be long before the warheads of the torpedos would begin to go. The sick and wounded had to be taken off. Any moment, Captain Sherman thought, the whole ship might go up in one big skyrocket of flame.

All was secured. By 1630 *Lexington* was stopped and all hands were prepared to abandon ship. Rafts were thrown over the side, and the 150 men wounded in action were taken off in baskets, lowered into whaleboats, and moved to other vessels. At 1707 Admiral Fitch decided to abandon. Men set their shoes in neat lines on the flight deck and climbed down the ropes into the water. The destroyers clustered around in the calm sea and picked the men up methodically; nobody was drowned or hurt in the abandonment.

As evening fell, Captain Sherman made a last inspection of the ship to see that no one had been left behind, and then prepared to go off the ship himself. His departure was accompanied by another explosion, as if to assure all that they had done what they had to do. And then, with everyone off the ship, Admiral Fletcher ordered the destroyer *Phelps* to do what must be done. She torpedoed the *Lexington*, which slipped down into 2400 fathoms of water, never to be seen again.

Both sides could claim victory in this battle, could they not?

The Japanese had sunk mighty *Lexington*, and the oiler *Neosho*, and the destroyer *Sims*. The Americans had sunk only *Shoho* and damaged *Shokaku*.

From the American point of view it was a victory because they had sunk their first enemy carrier, and by carrying the war to him, had prevented the invasion of Port Moresby. The Japanese lost an important ship to an American submarine, and they then learned that Hasley, with *Enterprise* and *Hornet*, was on his way to join *Yorktown*. That would give the Americans three carriers in the area, against Japan's one operable carrier, *Zuikaku*. So for the first time the Japanese navy retreated, and that was obviously an American victory.

But the real victory was more subtle, and was indicated by *Zuikaku*'s fate when she reached home a few days later. The high command in Tokyo put her up in mothballs, not because she was damaged, but because she had lost so many of her trained pilots that she was not considered a good fighting machine. This Japanese loss was to prove the most serious of the carrier war.

CHAPTER FOUR

Midway

The Japanese action in the Pacific war had been until now precisely as planned, although no one in Japan had expected the victories to come so easily or so quickly. The security perimeter would run from the Aleutian Islands in the north to Midway, Wake Island, the Marshalls, the Gilberts, the Solomons, New Caledonia, and Port Moresby. They hoped to force the Americans to sign a treaty establishing this perimeter of Japanese empire, and then settle down to promote the Greater East Asia Co-Prosperity Sphere, in which Japan would become the senior trading partner and from which the western powers would be prohibited.

Not being party to the Japanese plans, the Americans did not know that they had thrown two serious hitches into the scheme in recent weeks. First, and more important, was the Halsey-Doolittle raid on Tokyo. Second was the indefinite postponement of the invasion of Port Moresby, by which the Japanese had hoped to establish a southern anchor for the defense perimeter.

The Japanese had always planned to invade Midway and the Aleutians, but their timing was put off by the Tokyo Raid. Suddenly Admiral Yamamoto was faced with the fact that as things stood Japan was not immune to attack. So Midway must come next, and with it the simultaneous destruction of the American carrier force. Deprived of their carriers, the Americans would not move into the South Pacific, and the invasion of Port Moresby and establishment of the defense perimeter could be attempted again.

44

The operation would consist of three parts. First would be an invasion of the Aleutians. Second would be the occupation of Midway. Third would be the hovering about the area of the strong carrier striking force, which would be ready to smash the American fleet if that fleet could be persuaded to come out and do battle, as Admiral Yamamoto so fervently hoped.

Yamamoto's intelligence was somewhat lacking in May 1942. He believed the pilots' reports that they had sunk both *Lexington* and *Yorktown*. He also was contemptuous of the American power to act swiftly and strongly, and felt that he would lure the Americans out and then trap them in "jaws of steel."

Intelligence, on the other hand, was the most powerful weapon that Admiral Nimitz had at his disposal. The Americans had cracked the Japanese naval code, and were able to read the messages that went between fleet units. They were aware of the Japanese plans, strength, and disposition long before the ships neared Midway. Thus they could be waiting, not to be trapped, but to trap.

As for forces, the disparity was frightening. The Japanese would bring four carriers, two battleships, three cruisers, and fourteen destroyers in the striking force. The actual occupation force consisted of another two battleships, nine cruisers, one light carrier, eleven destroyers, and various other ships; the first force was set up solely to destroy the American fleet. Then there was what the Japanese called the "main body," consisting of more battleships, another light carrier, more cruisers and destroyers, which could be thrown into the Midway operation or the Aleutians.

Countering all this might, Admiral Nimitz had a thin gray line of ships at his disposal, very thin indeed, and as far as carriers were concerned the situation seemed almost hopeless. *Lexington* was sunk. *Saratoga*, now repaired, was in San Diego training air crews how to fight. *Yorktown* was damaged and had to go into the yard for repairs that Admiral Fitch estimated would take about three months.

When Nimitz learned of the Japanese intentions, he sent a hurry-up call for Halsey to come home from the South Pacific with *Enterprise* and *Hornet*, to provide his line of carriers to oppose the Japanese.

On May 25, the Japanese were ready to go. For ten days they had been moving to the staging area at Saipan, and aboard the superbattleship *Yamato* no less a personage than Admiral Yamamoto was preparing to lead the main body himself. Admiral Nagumo was there again, in *Akagi*; he had certainly shown his abilities at Pearl Harbor and thereafter, and now would give the coup de grâce to the American fleet.

In spite of what had happened to *Shokaku* and *Zuikaku* at the Battle of the Coral Sea, the Japanese were perfectly confident, even cocky. They were better trained than the Americans, and they knew they were pilots. The pilots had about 700 hours of flight time before going into carrier operations, as opposed to the Americans' 300 hours. The Japanese had better planes; their Zero was superior to the F4F, their torpedo bomber far surpassed the slow American TBD. Had not—as they believed—their Fifth Air Squadron sunk two American carriers in the Coral Sea? And was not the force going to Midway the pride of Japanese naval aviation? This force included the First and Second Air Squadrons, and their joke about the Fifth Squadron and the Americans was: "Sons of concubines won victory, so the sons of legal wives should find no rival in the world."

It was a gay party aboard the flagship that night of May 25, and the senior officers raised cups and upended them time after time. They praised the Emperor and themselves and the glory of the Japanese people, which would be established for 10,000 years after this coming victory at Midway. The next day was quiet, as some officers nursed their hangovers and others finished up the details of loading and storage for a long and dangerous voyage.

Yamato was anchored at Hashirajima anchorage, south of Hiroshima in the western Inland Sea, and around her were sixty-seven warships, the pride of the Combined Fleet. The lesser vessels and the troops for occupation, setting out from Saipan, would meet them in midocean.

At 0800 on May 27 the orders came, and aboard Admiral Nagumo's carrier force flagship the *Akagi* the flags began to flutter. It was time to set out for the historic battle. The ships were ready, their boilers superheated, and they began to slip away from the anchorage, past cheering fishermen in their little boats, escorted for a few miles by seaplanes from the naval base.

The admiral and his staff were assembled on *Akagi*'s bridge. The group included Comdr. Minoru Genda, the architect of the victory at Pearl Harbor, and Lt. Comdr. Mitsuo Fuchida, who had actually led the planes into battle that day. Fuchida in particular was irritable because he had a stomach ache and because he so disapproved of the haste with which this operation had been planned after the Doolittle raid had sent waves of shock throughout Japan. He did not like *Akagi*'s poor communications equipment, inferior for a flagship. He did not believe that the battleships would destroy the American fleet with the aid of the carriers; he suspected it was going to be just the other way around.

Fuchida had expected to play a major role in the coming battle in the air. That night of May 27 his hopes were blasted; he came down with an acute attack of appendicitis, and was taken to sick bay and operated on that very night. So he was out of it. Commander Genda, who was charged with responsibility for air operations, was worried about Admiral Nagumo's failure to take any initiative for planning this operation. It was almost as if Nagumo was passive about the prospects for victory or defeat. Genda and Fuchida both had commented on the looseness of security for the attack; everyone in Japan seemed to know that it was about to begin.

Overall, however, these worries and fears seemed insignificant, as the mighty Japanese fleet steamed on toward Midway.

At Midway, the defenders were warned that they could expect an attack early in June, for on May 25, Admiral Yamamoto's sailing orders had been picked up by the Americans at Pearl Harbor. The Combat Intelligence Unit at Pearl had already figured out where the attack would be, and now they knew the units involved. Admiral Nimitz could plan—but what had he to plan with?

On the morning of May 26, Bull Halsey came charging back to Pearl, hastened even faster than usual by Nimitz's message to "expedite return." Something was up, and Halsey knew it. But Halsey was to have no part of it; he got up out of his bunk that morning and went over to Nimitz' headquarters, and was promptly clapped into the hospital. He had a bad case of skin rash, brought on by nerves and strain during recent months.

Nimitz asked Halsey who should take over the task force, and Halsey named Rear Adm. Raymond Spruance, who had been with him as cruiser commander on a number of his raids. He could not have made a better choice, for Admiral Spruance was the coolest strategist in the Pacific. That very day, as soon as he was notified of the appointment, he went to see Nimitz and they began talking about the plan. There was only one way, said Spruance: take the carriers out northeast of Midway and lie in wait and ambush the Japanese as they came in. The Japanese would not know that the Americans had broken the code and were tipped off to the invasion. Yamamoto and Nagumo would believe that only when they began their attack would the American fleet come out to fight. The element of surprise must be used for all it was worth, because what else did they have? At that moment they had *Enterprise* and *Hornet*. Fletcher was coming back in *Yorktown*, but from what Fitch had reported back at Coral Sea, it was doubtful if *Yorktown* could go into battle in sixty days, let alone in a week or so.

Task Force 17 arrived that afternoon, *Yorktown* trailing the oil slick of an injured ship as she had all across the ocean. They put her into drydock, and the yard officials came down to look and estimate the number of weeks it would take to repair her.

"We must have this ship back in three days," Nimitz said in his quiet way.

In the fleet nobody believed it was possible, but Nimitz knew, and he told Spruance as the junior admiral got ready to steam that *Yorktown* would join them at sea.

So on the morning of May 28, Task Force 16 sailed, with Admiral Spruance, known in the fleet as a "battleship admiral" walking the bridge that Bull Halsey had trod for so long.

He did, however, have Halsey's staff, and particularly Captain Miles Browning, a brilliant, nervous, irascible career aviator.

The two forces, American and Japanese steamed toward Midway. On May 29 and 30 the Japanese began to encounter bad weather, rain and heavy winds that cut their speed and wasted their fuel. Aboard the flagship the communications officers noted heavy traffic between Radio Pearl and Midway and wondered if the invasion force had been spotted somehow. But Admiral Yamamoto did not believe it had, and did not worry.

On May 31 the carrier forces of Admiral Nagumo met the bad weather. This day the traffic with Midway was even heavier, and Admiral Yamamoto hoped the American fleet might be getting ready to come out. He should know soon, he said, because he had sent ahead a half dozen long-range flying boats to scout out the enemy. But the Japanese planes, which were to center on French Frigate Shoals, arrived and found American planes there, so they had to abandon that mission. Yamamoto lost his "eyes."

The weather grew worse for the Japanese. On June 1 and 2 they fueled. That day a Japanese patrol plane encountered an American flying boat about 700 miles off Midway, and they exchanged gunfire. Each side, then, was alerted to the presence of the other, but of course the Japanese did not know of the approach of the carriers *Enterprise* and *Hornet* to the area.

And *Yorktown* was coming too. The men of the repair yard had done the impossible: they had the big carrier ready for action in three days. She had sailed from Pearl Harbor on May 30 and, after fueling, the whole American force had come together on June 2, in weather almost as bad as that which bedeviled the Japanese.

On the Japanese carriers, the pilots played *hanafuda* for cigarettes and listened to records. On the American carriers, the pilots played rummy and poker for money, and listened to records. The Japanese had known for days where they were going and what they were going to do. The Americans were told the defense plan on June 1, when no man could accidentally betray it; again, secrecy was the Americans' best weapon.

The morning of June 3 dawned sloppy for the Japanese, and spotty for the Americans. But on Midway itself operations began as usual with take-off of the PBY patrol planes at 0415. The planes moved out in a great circle, 400 miles from Midway, and found nothing. Then, just after nine o'clock in the morning, two patrol planes almost simultaneously came upon elements of the Japanese fleet.

"Do you see what I see?" said one pilot to his copilot.

"You're damned right I do," was the answer.

And below, a Japanese cruiser fired a smoke shell to tell the fleet that there above them hovered a PBY.

From Midway, nine B-17 bombers set out to attack the Japanese fleet; they found the fleet, dropped their bombs, but scored nothing but a near miss on a freighter. PBYs attacked with torpedoes and hit one tanker of the invasion transport convoy. But that was all.

At 1800, the three American carriers were 300 miles northeast of Midway, about 400 miles away from the Japanese carriers. On the night of June 3 the two forces were steaming on courses that would bring them together just northwest of Midway. Admiral Fletcher, the senior American officer, was in command. He was waiting for the Japanese to launch an air attack on Midway the next morning.

He was not disappointed.

At 0300 the Japanese were ready to launch planes from the carriers *Akagi* and *Kaga, Soryu,* and *Hiryu.* Aboard *Akagi,* a fretful Lt. Comdr. Fuchida watched as the planes warmed up. First came the search planes, launched at 0430, and the attack wave against Midway. Lt. Joichi Tomonaga led this first attack wave. The Zeros streamed by, gunning their engines one after another and swooping up off the flight decks. Then came the dive-bombers, carrying 500-pound bombs—in all, 108 planes to hit the island and knock out its defenses.

No sooner had the first wave gotten off *Akagi* and the other carriers than the order came to prepare the second wave. Bells clanged and the elevators groaned as they brought the planes up from the hangar deck to spot them for take-off, forward elevators carrying fighters and the midship and stern elevators bringing bombers. This wave would carry bombs and torpedoes.

Patrol planes from Midway discovered the first wave and the Japanese carriers around 0530, and the word began to go out. It was delayed in reaching Admiral Fletcher and he did not get it until 0600, but then he radioed Admiral Spruance to move southwest and attack the carriers. Task Force 16 plunged ahead at twenty-five knots; the alarms began to sound on *Enterprise* and *Hornet* and men began to scramble down to the ready rooms.

At 0616 the Japanese were approaching Midway when suddenly they were jumped by American fighters, which swooped down, guns blazing, and shot down two of *Hiryu*'s bombers before the Japanese were scarcely aware of the coming of the Americans. But the American fighter pilots were flying F4Fs and ancient Buffaloes that could not compete with the fast Zeroes. The Japanese fighters drove off the Americans, but not without heavy losses. The Americans suffered too, and after the first attack was over very few of the fighters were able to get back into the air.

The first wave's attack on the islands of this atoll was over before 0700, and the six remaining American fighters straggled in. They counted noses: two flyable planes left of the twenty-five that had gone after the Japanese.

At 0705 a bugle sounded the air raid alarm aboard the Japanese carriers. Six American TBFs and four B-26 bombers were coming in, all armed with torpedoes. Admiral Nagumo looked up as a destroyer began firing antiaircraft shells at the planes. The black smoke puffs surrounded the planes, which came in from two different directions. The cruisers began firing, and then the battleship *Kirishima* opened up with her rough bark. The bursts were all around the American planes, but none of them went down. Then the Zero fighters, which had been hovering above the fleet, swooped into their own antiaircraft fire and began pressing an attack. Soon three American planes were on fire and crashing. Three more came on in and released their torpedoes; one passed over *Akagi*, nearly grazing the bridge before it plunged into the sea.

The torpedo wakes came close by *Akagi*, but she maneuvered out of the way and escaped. The admiral and his staff breathed a sigh of relief. At about this time, Lieutenant Tomonaga reported that another air strike was needed at Midway. Admiral Nagumo, who had been ducking on his bridge, did not need to be convinced further. He ordered another strike on the island.

Now the Japanese had a new problem. *Akagi* and *Kaga* had loaded the bombers with torpedoes for use against the enemy fleet when it was found. Those torpedoes had to be unloaded and replaced with bombs. Precious minutes were wasted as the planes were taken below, the arms removed, and the bombs brought on.

As this was going on, the force was attacked again, by fourteen B-17s that had taken off from Midway before dawn. The bombers came in at 20,000 feet, dropped their bombs, all of which missed, and sped away. On the bridge of *Akagi* Lieutenant Commander Fuchida fretted because no Japanese fighters went up after the big American planes.

Now came another group of American planes, sixteen dive-bombers, which came in to skip-bomb because the pilots had not yet had enough training in dive-bombing technique. Eight of these were shot down, and the rest were almost all casualties on landing back at Midway.

By this time the Japanese in the attack force had become contemptuous of the American attackers. Lieutenant Tomonaga returned with his first wave, and they began to land. Some pilots were wounded—Lt. Hiroharu Kadono, who had been hit in the leg, and despite loss of blood made his way back to *Kiryu* and landed, collapsed in a dead faint the moment his plane stopped on the flight deck. Tomonaga spoke of the attack, and was ready to go into detail for Admiral Nagumo, but the admiral had a great deal else on his mind right then.

In the midst of the attacks from the Midway-based planes came a report to the flagship that an enemy task force had been sighted 240 miles from Midway. When Admiral Nagumo got the word, he was shocked; how could the Americans have responded so quickly to the attack? No one in the Japanese fleet had expected the Americans to come out so soon. And now the enemy was just 200 miles away! Admiral Nagumo countermanded the order to load the planes with bombs. They must be armed now with weapons to strike an enemy fleet. The rearming was already half-finished; now it had to be undone.

Nagumo was plagued by bad intelligence this morning. What kind of ships were in the enemy force? He asked and asked again, but had no answer until 0809, when he was told they were five cruisers and five destroyers. But eleven minutes later he learned that there was at least one carrier among the ships.

Admiral Nagumo hesitated. From *Hiryu* came the suggestion of Rear Adm. Tamon Yamaguchi: "Consider it advisable to launch attack force immediately."

The message reached the flagship, but Admiral Kusaka, the chief of staff, thought it the headstrong advice of a hot young air admiral and much too dangerous to follow. And so the process was delayed. The planes on the carriers were gassed and armed and made ready. It was estimated that they would be ready to take off about 1100.

"After completing homing operations, proceed northward," Admiral Nagumo told his fleet confidently. "We plan to contact and destroy the enemy task force."

To do so, Admiral Nagumo would use eighteen torpedo planes from *Akagi*, twenty-seven from *Kaga*, thirty-six dive-bombers from *Hiryu* and *Soryu*, and three fighters from each carrier. That ought to be enough to wipe out the insolent Americans.

But Admiral Nagumo did not know precisely *how* insolent those Americans could be. He was about to learn.

On the morning of June 4, the American carrier force had her patrols out; Admiral Fletcher wanted to recover them before launching a strike, so he told Admiral Spruance to maneuver to attack. Spruance began to move. He planned to launch at 0900. The ships went to general quarters as they searched for the enemy; that would give them a flight of only about 100 miles to hit the enemy, well within the 175-mile radius of the American planes. But Captain Browning had another idea: if they would launch early, quite probably they could catch the Japanese cold turkey, with their carriers' decks full of planes returned from the strike against Midway. At least they would have the element of surprise. It was risky, because it would make full use of the planes' flight radius, allowing virtually nothing for error. But risk was the order of the day; all Spruance had to do was contemplate the disparity in forces, which he knew well from his briefings at Pearl Harbor on the basis of the broken Japanese code. The Americans had to take advantage of every break, indeed had to make their own breaks, to win this struggle today. And if they did not win it, they must lose it; the problem was as simple as that.

So Spruance, the battleship admiral, saw the sense of the big gamble Captain Browning was offering, and he behaved just as Halsey would have behaved: he took the gamble, accepting the grave risks.

Planes began launching from *Enterprise* at 0702. It would be the full shake: every operational plane except those needed for Combat Air Patrol would go on the mission—twenty fighters, sixty-seven dive-bombers, and twenty-nine torpedo bombers would make the effort.

The pilots climbed to 19,000 feet and then began heading in the general direction of the Japanese carriers. They did not know precisely where the enemy could be found, but they were on their way, searching. The change in course ordered by Nagumo to intercept the Americans caused *Hornet*'s attack group commander to miss the Japanese, and thus *Hornet*'s pilots missed the battle, some making it to Midway to land, and many ditching in the sea. Yet not all *Hornet*'s planes would miss the fight. Lt. Comdr. John C. Waldron was leading Torpedo Squadron 8. Waldron was a fine officer and a fine pilot, and he knew better than anyone in his group how poor was the airplane with which he had to fight. In fact, he did not expect to come back alive, and was doubtful if any of his squadron would return. He was determined, however, to press the attack and do as much damage as he could.

Waldron found the Japanese just before 0930, first as two columns of smoke on the horizon, and then as individual ships, the four carriers in two lines in the middle. Fifteen planes, slow and unresponsive planes by modern standards, headed directly toward the enemy to launch their torpedoes.

Aboard the Japanese carriers, the pilots were to take off for a strike against the Americans at 1030, and were spotted on the decks. Then the antiaircraft guns of the outer ships began to pop, and a message came back to the admiral on the *Akagi*. Nagumo sent out the order to speed preparations for take-off; he knew as well as anyone what it would be like to be caught by enemy bombers with a deckload of planes.

On *Akagi* Lieutenant Commander Fuchida watched as little specks appeared in the sky; they were eight miles out from the fleet when the Japanese gunners opened up. The planes waggled their wings and headed in on *Akagi*'s starboard bow. Up above, the Japanese Zeros swooped down and began knocking off the bombers, one by one; the Zeros were too fast for the old ships. To the right and left of Waldron they went down; then his plane was hit, and he took the long plunge into the sea. Soon only three were left, and then there was one, piloted by Ens. George Gay. He bored in, heading for a carrier, released his torpedo, and headed across the flight deck of another carrier to escape. The Zeros got him; they had already shot his gunner, but Gay managed to ditch and then hide beneath a seat cushion in the water. He was the sole survivor of Torpedo Squadron 8, which had not put a single "fish" into a Japanese ship. It was hardly surprising—the Japanese had put up fifty Zeros against the clumsy bombers.

A few minutes later the torpedo bombers of *Enterprise*'s Torpedo Squadron 6 came lumbering in. The story was much the same, although the slaughter was not so severe since many Zeros had landed on their carriers to refuel. Lt. Comdr. Eugene Lindsey, squadron commander, was shot down, along with nine others of the fourteen who made the raid. None of their torpedoes hit either.

At 0936 it seemed that it was all over. The Japanese carrier men regarded with some contempt the techniques and skills of their enemy. The Americans had sent six attacks against the striking force that morning, and except for damaging one ship, they had scored nothing more than near misses by bombardment, although they had killed and wounded many men by strafing. Still, it was the ships that counted this day, and the ships were safe and sound. Or were they? The Japanese thought they were safe, and now that the enemy was disposed of, stopped the radical maneuvering that had occupied the carriers for the past half hour and set about the business of launching the counterstrike. One after the other planes were brought up from the hangars and spotted. At 1020 Admiral Nagumo gave the order to launch when ready. *Akagi* and the other carriers turned into the wind to launch. On the flight decks the propellers of the planes were spinning as the pilots warmed their engines. In five minutes all the planes would be launched against the Americans.

At 1024 on *Akagi*, Lieutenant Commander Fuchida heard the order on the bridge to launch. The air officer flapped his flag, and a Zero began moving down the deck. And just then someone shouted: "Hell-divers!"

Fuchida looked up and saw three black spots darting downward toward the *Akagi*. The same sight was duplicated on the other three Japanese carriers, for the American dive-bombers had found them.

Lt. Comdr. Clarence McClusky was leading the dive-bombers from *Enterprise*. He split them, half taking *Kaga*, and the other half diving on *Akagi*. It was the bombers led by Lt. R. H. Best that Fuchida saw as black specks moving down. There was no interference. The Japanese fighters had come down low to knock off the torpedo planes, and had not been able to climb back, so the bombers hurtled in. *Akagi* had forty planes on deck; Fuchida heard the "terrifying scream," then the crash of a direct hit on the carrier, then a blinding flash and a second louder explosion, and finally a third, lesser one. He looked around and saw a huge hole in the flight deck, just behind the amidships elevator. The elevator was twisted and falling into the hangar deck. Deckplates were standing on end and planes were belching fire and crumbling. He staggered down into the ready room, and then climbed back up to the bridge, where he could see that *Kaga* and *Soryu* had also been hit and were burning.

The brilliance of Captain Browning's guess was made clear. *Akagi* herself had not been so badly injured by the three bombs, but the bombs did set fire to the planes on the deck, planes loaded with torpedoes, and the torpedoes began to explode, driving the fire-fighters away. The fire spread down into the hangar deck, caught more planes, and spread toward the bridge.

Admiral Nagumo seemed stunned. His staff officers pleaded with him to transfer his flag to the cruiser *Nagara,* but he did not want to leave *Akagi.* The damage control officer came up from below and reported that all the passages below were on fire and that they must escape quickly if at all. The admiral had to climb out the bridge window and down a rope ladder to the anchor deck, where he could get into a boat from *Nagara.*

Captain Aoki, Fuchida, and a handful of others remained on the bridge of *Akagi,* but Fuchida followed his admiral down to the anchor deck, and was taken by stretcher to the cruiser. Captain Aoki fought the fires for hours, but it was no use. *Akagi* was doomed.

McClusky, along with eight other planes, had dived on *Kaga,* carrying 1,000-pound and 500-pound bombs. At least four of these bombs hit and did tremendous damage—one killed the captain of the ship and nearly everyone else on the bridge, leaving as senior officer the air officer, Comdr. Takahisa Amagai. She burned, and after three and a half hours was dead in the water. As with *Akagi,* the portrait of the Emperor was transferred from the ship, but men stayed on to fight the fires until the very end.

Lt. Comdr. M. F. Leslie led the dive-bombers of *Yorktown* against the third carrier, *Soryu.* He caught her with her planes ready to take off, and hit the flight deck with three bombs from the seventeen dive-bombers. The entire ship burst into flames, and within twenty minutes *Soryu* carrier was abandoned. Not one of these American bombers was touched, but on the way home the Americans were chased fiercely by the Zeros, and most of them escaped by going down "on the deck" and staying there. There were some heroic actions here. McClusky's radio mechanic shot down one Zero with his machine gun. The gunner on another dive-bomber hung on to his gun after it had broken loose from the mount, laid it on the fuselage, and shot down a Zero that was chasing the plane.

The American attack was all over then, and the planes that were ever going back to the carriers were home shortly after noon. The cost had been high: *Enterprise* had lost fourteen of her thirty-seven dive-bombers, ten of fourteen torpedo planes, and one fighter. *Hornet* had lost all her torpedo bombers and eleven fighters. *Yorktown* had lost all but one of her fourteen torpedo bombers, two dive-bombers and, three fighters. But three Japanese carriers were burning and would sink before the battle ended.

Of all the Japanese carriers only *Hiryu* was left, and she was as dangerous as ever, particularly because Admiral Yamaguchi, her commander, was an aggressive fighter. By eleven o'clock she launched eighteen dive-bombers and six fighters and sent them off to find *Yorktown,* whose general whereabouts had been reported earlier to the Japanese fleet. Just before noon the planes arrived over the carrier and moved in to attack. Admiral Fletcher was on his bridge, wearing a tin hat as the fight raged in the air above him. Only nine of the dive-bombers got through, and then another was knocked down, but three bombs fell on the carrier, and caused substantial damage, so that the magazines were flooded to prevent her blowing up. One fire on the island, the bridge network, knocked out the communications of the ship, so Fletcher transferred to the cruiser *Astoria.* The fire-fighters worked on the carrier, but another wave of *Hiryu*'s bombers got through; this time they were torpedo planes. *Yorktown* managed to dodge most of them, but two hit her and caused her to list severely to port. She was abandoned because her captain feared she might capsize.

That afternoon, at 1530, Admiral Spruance ordered another attack on the Japanese from *Enterprise,* and twenty-four dive-bombers jumped *Hiryu* an hour and a half later. They did to her what they had done to the other three carriers, although the Japanese ship maneuvered at thirty knots in a desperate attempt to squirm away. She never made it. Four bombs hit her, knocked out the island, and started fires that could not be controlled. Soon she was far behind the fleet, with two destroyers standing by her, and it was apparent she would be lost.

Admiral Yamamoto received the bad news as these battles raged. He was unable to accept it for what it was; the shock was too great for Japan. For months now the Japanese had moved so swiftly, and gained so much contempt for the soft ways of the westerners, that it was hard to believe these same westerners were able to stand up and fight on Japan's own terms—and win. Admiral Nagumo had no such illusions: he had spent much of the day ducking American planes that whizzed by his flag bridge, and he had seen Americans make the supreme sacrifice of their lives by flying in steadily in antiquated aircraft under murderous antiaircraft fire and Zero pursuit. But Yamamoto was far from the battle, and he could still delude himself.

So that night, these orders went out to the fleet: "The enemy fleet is practically destroyed and is withdrawing eastward. The Combined Fleet is preparing to pursue the survivors and to occupy Midway. The Battle Fleet will arrive at midnight at [he gave the coordinates in midocean].... The Mobile Force, the Occupation Force ... and the submarines are ordered to seek contact with the enemy and to attack him."

Nagumo knew. In fact, he was now convinced that the American fleet was much more powerful than it actually was. "The total enemy force is five aircraft carriers, six cruisers and fifteen destroyers," he replied to Yamamoto. "We are protecting *Hiryu* and will withdraw toward the northwest at eighteen knots."

An hour later, Nagumo reported again: "The enemy still has four aircraft carriers, six cruisers, and fifteen destroyers. None of our aircraft carriers is seaworthy."

At last Yamamoto understood. He also made Nagumo the scapegoat, relieving him of command and substituting Admiral Kondo, commander of the second fleet, in command of the striking force.

Kondo decided he would seek a night engagement with the Americans in an effort to even the score. The Japanese had studied night fighting and trained for it for several years, and were notably superior to the Americans in technique and ability. Kondo hoped to get in with his battleships and cruisers and smash the carriers.

But Yamamoto had second thoughts. If the Japanese pressed east, the Americans with their "four carriers" could launch a massive air strike against them at dawn, and what was now disaster might become total rout. So just before three o'clock on the morning of June 5, Admiral Yamamoto ordered the general retirement of the Midway invasion force and the striking force. He had lost all four of his fast carriers, all their planes, and nearly all their pilots.

The loss of Lieutenant Tomonaga of *Hiryu* illustrates what had happened, and what would happen in this carrier war. Tomonaga's plane had been hit in the port wing tank during the battle over Midway and needed repairs. But when the order came for the second wave of *Hiryu* planes to take off, Tomonaga ordered his mechanic to get the plane lined up for take-off. The mechanic informed him that the port tank had not been repaired.

"Too bad," said Tomonaga. "Just fill the starboard one."

And he took off, knowing that he would not have the fuel to get back to his carrier.

That tale made Tomonaga a hero of the Japanese, and illustrated the *Bushido* spirit that was later to lead such Japanese pilots to suicide missions. But in fact it would not have made any difference if Tomonaga's port tank had been repaired, because by the time he could come home there was nothing to come home to. And here was the loss that Japan found irreparable—the loss of the valiant First and Second Air Squadrons. For the entire rest of the carrier war Japan would not recover the advantage she had in the early months, when her highly trained pilots ran rings around the Americans.

Midway marked the change in the war that Yamamoto had feared would come. The Japanese had been stopped at Coral Sea, and now defeated at Midway. Admiral Spruance had shown himself to be a cool commander who was able to handle a carrier force as well as cruisers or battleships. And so Midway marked the turning point of the Pacific War, as well as the unshakable realization that the aircraft carrier was the weapon that would decide the struggle when navies met.

CHAPTER FIVE

South Pacific

A few weeks after the battle of Midway, the Joint Chiefs of Staff of the United States decided it was time to strike back on land, and they picked as the first point of American offensive the South Pacific, where Japan was extended and where there was a threat to Australia and the whole American effort to rebuild.

In August 1942, the United States Marines landed in the Solomon Islands, and a wearing, dreadful battle began. To support the land forces and fight against the Japanese air bases around these islands, the navy sent three carriers to the South Pacific under Vice Adm. Frank Jack Fletcher, who was senior airman now that Halsey was sick—although actually he was not an airman at all. He had *Saratoga*, *Enterprise*, and the newer carrier *Wasp*. They covered the landings and protected the transports from Japanese air attack.

For this operation *Enterprise* was under the command of Capt. Arthur C. Davis, an experienced officer whose elevation represented the coming of the new breed of carrier men. The carrier had a new air officer too, Comdr. John Crommelin, a light haired southerner and a veteran fighter pilot. She had a new admiral aboard, Rear Adm. Thomas C. Kinkaid—he would command the task force built around the carrier. On July 15, *Enterprise* had sailed for this action in the south, working up all the way south. Commander Crommelin sent his pilots out on 200-mile searches, and those planes that were not engaged in search were involved in training flights. The new torpedo planes and the bombers made run after run on towed targets, to practice for what was coming.

The force was formed on July 26, southeast of the Fiji Islands, *Enterprise* meeting *Wasp* and *Saratoga* and the other ships. Then came the invasion.

The carriers' job this day was to support the landing. At 0515 the order was given to start engines, and the planes began coughing blue smoke and warming up on the flight deck. An hour before sunrise *Enterprise* and the other carriers were launching their planes, first F4F fighters, and then SBD dive-bombers carrying 1,000-pound bombs. They moved into the beaches at Tulagi and dropped bombs and strafed, preparing the way for the Marines. By seven o'clock in the morning this phase of the work was over, and the Marines in their gray-green were moving in to shore, with planes above them and the troops going into Guadalcanal.

All morning long it was quiet in the air. No Japanese planes appeared, and the Americans suffered no losses. It was almost eerie, because the Japanese had plenty of force in the area, land-based air-power and carriers too. The quiet lasted until half an hour after noon.

Then the radar men on *Enterprise* warned their pilots: a large "bogey"—a force of unidentified aircraft—was approaching from the northwest. That was the area from which the Japanese were most likely to arrive. They did not find their enemy, but they were coming in nonetheless, and they came fast, a swarm of them moving in a V-shape, thirty twin-engined bombers surrounded by a flock of Zero fighters.

Lt. Vincent DePoix of *Enterprise* saw them and closed in with three other fighters. He fired a long burst, and one enemy bomber rolled out of formation and crashed into the sea north of Florida Island. Then the fracas began. Two other *Enterprise* pilots attacked from above, darting down on the opposite sides of the bombers, and another bomber began to smoke and dropped out of formation. Then the Zeros hied to mix it up, those fast Japanese fighters that could outturn and outfly the F4Fs. Two Zeros got after DePoix, and he squirmed away. Another Zero attacked one of DePoix's mates, and he hit on its tail and gave it a long burst. The Zero pulled into a dive and disappeared, but just then the pilot, Machinist J.A. Achten, saw 20-mm. cannon holes appearing in his right wing, and he pulled away. The enemy pilot was determined, the dogfight continued, and Achten's plane began to respond like a sick bird. He was lucky; he found a cumulus cloud and dived in to shake off the pursuer.

The other American pilots had the same luck—the Zeros were too much, and all of the Americans escaped into the clouds and nursed their planes back to the carrier, shot full of holes.

That was the end of American air supremacy over Guadal-canal for quite a while. The rest of that day the pilots of *Enterprise* and the other carriers were fighting for their lives, and to knock down the bombers that threatened the American troops below. Another group from *Enterprise* found these same bombers and chased them, but each time they attacked the more maneuverable Zeros were after them, driving them away. Lt. (jg.) R.E. Rhodes got involved with four Zeros and scrambled like a wildcat to shoot down one and then escape into a cloud before the others could get him. Three fighters from *Enterprise* did not come home from this chase.

On the afternoon of this first day of the American invasion, the Japanese sent over dive-bombers to smash the American ships unloading supplies, and the pilots of Fighting 6, *Enterprise*'s Fighter Squadron, went after them. Lt. A.O. Vorse shot down one dive-bomber that went straight down into Iron Bottom Sound. At two o'clock in the afternoon a flight of F4Fs caught bombers over Beach Red on Guadalcanal Island, and shot down one, then another, and then two more as they hit the deck and ran for safer territory. The score looked very good. Later in the day F4Fs drove after a group of low-flying Japanese torpedo bombers that moved in from the north across the eastern tip of Florida Island, bombers flying so low that their propellers kicked up spray on the blue water below. There were twenty-six of these Japanese planes, covered by Zeros, but the American fighters went after them. The Japanese sent one torpedo into the destroyer *Jarvis*, but the Americans sank nearly all the torpedo planes.

It was apparent what the carrier planes could do. But that day, August 8, Admiral Fletcher became worried because his carriers were exposed in these restricted waters. He moved away after two days of supporting the American landings, and by moving left the land forces and the naval forces in the area at the mercy of Japanese air and naval superiority. The Japanese did not need long to take advantage of their opportunity. On August 9, a Japanese fleet moved down into the area and smashed the Americans, sinking four Allied cruisers and damaging a fifth so badly that it was not of use for a long time. This was a lesson in the absence of air power.

After Admiral Fletcher moved the carriers away from the scene of action, they carried out routine patrols for the next two weeks.

Admiral Yamamoto was hastening to put together a force that could retake the islands from the Americans, and in the third week in August a force of forty-nine Japanese warships, with the carriers *Shokaku, Zuikaku,* and *Ryujo,* headed south. By this time the Americans had captured a good part of Guadalcanal Island, including Henderson Field, the vital airfield that was the reason both Americans and Japanese wanted Guadalcanal. The American hold was tenuous, the Japanese from Rabaul and other islands came in and bombed the field almost at will, and Japanese troops were still around the perimeter, but the Americans had Henderson Field, at least for the moment. Yamamoto was determined they should not keep it.

Yamamoto planned to sacrifice the small carrier *Ryujo* if necessary so the big carriers could knock out the Americans' big carriers. He sent out flying boats and other scouts ahead of the sea force. They were discovered by the Americans. By the evening of August 22, Admiral Fletcher knew that the enemy was coming, and the next morning Captain Davis had the word that Japanese transports loaded with reinforcement were headed for the beach at Guadalcanal, but the search planes did not find the enemy.

On August 24, patrol planes discovered *Ryujo* early in the afternoon, and *Enterprise* sent a force of scouts out. They found the carrier and bombed, but she maneuvered out of the way of the planes. The Japanese were advertising her—but they were not failing to protect her. All the American scouts that came after her were attacked by Zeros; one was shot down, and the others came home full of the holes that were the trademark of the Zero pilots. But then, Big E's planes also found *Shokaku* and *Zuikaku*. Lt. Ray Davis, commanding officer of Bombing 6, made the discovery on a search flight. Suddenly down below he spotted *Shokaku*, her flight deck filled with planes and men getting them ready, and *Zuikaku* five miles astern. Followed by his wingman, Ens. R.C. Shaw, Davis moved in to attack, although his squadron was carrying only 500-pound bombs. As they dived, the tracers sped up to meet them, and the puffs of antiaircraft fire clustered around their wings. At 5,000 feet Davis sighted through his bomb-sight; at 2,000 feet he pulled the bomb release, then levelled off, pulling out through seven planes that crisscrossed around the carrier. No hits, two near misses—one of them by not more than five feet.

Davis sent a message to *Enterprise*, but the ship did not hear it. Instead the message was relayed slowly by other planes, and so by the time Admiral Fletcher learned of the location of the two big Japanese carriers he had fallen into Yamamoto's trap—and had committed the planes of *Saratoga* to bombing *Ryujo*. And they did. They moved in force and smashed the little carrier and most of her planes, sending them down to the bottom of the sea.

But now the price was to be paid. *Shokaku* and *Zuikaku* launched their fighters and bombers against the American carriers.

Aboard *Enterprise*, the air crackled with tension. Above, the bedspring antenna searched the skies, stopping occasionally for a fix on some disturbance. Suddenly, at 1632, the antenna stopped, swung a little further, and then swung back—as the operator caught a glimpse of a huge formation of bogies moving in. Here it was, the Japanese counterattack.

The fighter directors sent their fighters out to intercept the Japanese. Four planes from one section saw a force coming, eighteen dive-bombers in one group, eighteen dive-bombers in another, both groups surrounded by Zeros. The American fighters moved to attack, although the Japanese were 10,000 feet higher than they. They slammed in after them, engaged, and split away to try to get at the bombers, but the Zeros came around again and the fight was on. This section, headed by Lt. Albert Vorse, shot down a Zero and a Messerschmitt 109, a German plane that oddly enough was out here in the Pacific. Then the section suddenly ran out of fuel and had to scuttle for *Saratoga*, the sister carrier, to try to land. Three of the four landed safely. Lieutenant Vorse landed in the wake of the carrier and was picked up by a destroyer. Scratch one more fighter.

The Japanese tried the reverse of the technique the Americans had used successfully at Midway. While the American fighters were up high engaging the Zeros and the dive-bombers, a force of torpedo bombers tried to sneak in very low on the water. But they reckoned without the American radar, which picked them up sixty miles out. A patrol section was vectored out to the area and found the Japanese planes unescorted. They shot down two torpedo planes, another bomber, and chased six bombers back toward the Japanese carriers.

The high-altitude fight was raging nearly over *Enterprise*, with the F4Fs and Zeros circling and shooting, and the Japanese bombers trying to get a shot at the carrier. Machinist Donald Runyon led one fighter into those bombers. He flashed down from 18,000 feet out of the sun and caught one, shot it up and saw it explode in midair. He then turned into the sun and back again, flaming a second dive-bomber with incendiaries. Then a Japanese plane came after him, trying the same tactic, and the whirlwind was working. The Japanese pilot overshot. Runyon had a quick glimpse of the enemy, fired, and the Zero began to burn. Then Runyon came up underneath a fourth plane, another bomber, and burned it. A Zero came after him and he shot this one up badly enough that the pilot took his smoking plane away from the fight. Meanwhile Runyon's three mates were shooting too, and damaged four more bombers, driving two others off.

Down below all this, *Enterprise* was steaming at twenty-seven knots, her big and small antiaircraft guns trained and ready for action, her crew at battle stations, watching for whatever they could see. Then, a few minutes after five o'clock, a sailor saw the flash of sun on a wing as a Japanese dive-bomber nosed over to come in on the ship. Antiaircraft guns opened up from the carrier and from the battleship *North Carolina* steaming near her. In spite of the working over by the American fighters, the Japanese were coming in, some thirty dive-bombers concentrating against *Enterprise*.

At 1713 *Enterprise* was under attack, bombers coming in on the port quarter. The men on the bridge maneuvered the ship, turning her and straightening her out, changing the pattern, providing as elusive a target as possible. On the decks the gunners strained and fired and fired again. The bombs began bursting around the carrier, sending huge inverted funnels up from the sea, and around the ship blossomed fountains of gasoline-fed flame as planes plunged into the water.

1714: the first bomb hit. Captain Davis had maneuvered skillfully, but this one came in and crashed through the forward starboard part of the after elevator, and down forty-two feet through the elevator well and three decks before exploding 1,000 pounds of TNT in a steel case.

Forward, men were thrown from their seats or knocked off their feet. In the area of the bomb thirty-five men were dead, killed by explosion and debris, and on the flight deck there was a bulge two feet high. Fires were started in mattresses in the berthing compartments, and holes in the hull let water come charging into the storage compartments, so that the *Enterprise* began to list.

1715: the second bomb hit. It fell within fifteen feet of the first, meaning disaster. Damage control crews came up and found that their hoses would not pull water—a rupture in a main had knocked out the pressure. Rivets popped, doors sprung, and another thirty-nine men were dead, some of them blown completely to pieces by the blast. This bomb was more dangerous to the ship's defense than the first, for it knocked out the guns on the starboard quarter.

And yet *Enterprise* steamed on at twenty-seven knots, and

the remaining guns gave forth a comforting barrage against the enemy.

1716: the third bomb. This bomb carried an instantaneous fuse and exploded on the flight deck, just aft of the carrier's island, blowing a ten-foot hole in the deck and putting the elevator there out of commission. But that was minor damage compared to what the other two bombs had done.

That was the end of the torture for *Enterprise*. Her own planes had saved her. The last dive-bomber to come into range had dropped its wicked concoction of explosive and steel, and the Japanese headed home.

Still, *Enterprise* was in trouble. She had serious fires, and they had to be controlled. But an hour after that third bomb hit, *Enterprise* was heading into the wind, recovering her planes. Then the steering broke down and she slowed to ten knots. Just then the Japanese chose to send in another strike. But as the radar men watched the screen, the Japanese sped by, fifty miles away, missing the carrier, and she was saved.

She had a good deal of trouble yet that evening. Some of her planes were out searching for the Japanese carriers. They did not find them, but they came back late, out of gas, to land in the darkness around ten o'clock that night. Two landed safely, but a third flew into the island and fouled the flight deck so that the remaining planes had to land on the *Saratoga*. They landed on the other carrier safely and were saved.

The next day *Enterprise* buried her dead and headed back for Pearl Harbor and basic repairs. Except for enough planes to fly patrol on the voyage, her air group was scattered among *Saratoga, Wasp,* and Henderson Field, for the Americans could not afford to let a single plane get away in these days of need.

That left *Saratoga* and *Wasp* for air defense against the Japanese fleet. But not for long. Southeast of Guadalcanal, early in the morning hours of August 31, the Japanese submarine *I-26* tracked *Saratoga* and put a torpedo into her. Twelve men were wounded, including Admiral Fletcher, but *Saratoga* did not go down. Still, she had to go for repairs, so her fliers too were decanted to Henderson Field, and the carrier headed for the yard.

That left *Wasp*.

The battle for Guadalcanal raged on and the Japanese brought down what became known as the Tokyo Express. Every night fast destroyers came into the waters of Guadalcanal, carrying troops and supplies for the Japanese who were trying to reconquer the island. They were effective and dangerous, and a grave trial to the Americans fighting on the island.

The Japanese did not commit the big carriers to action now, but held them off as threats to the Americans. By this time, *Hornet* had been brought down to the South Pacific to even up the carrier odds a bit, and she and *Wasp* were assigned to convoy duty, to protect American transports from the enemy.

On September 14 a convoy headed for Guadalcanal to reinforce the island garrison, if one could call it a garrison yet. On September 15, *Wasp* was responsible for combat air patrol and antisubmarine patrol, and her planes launched just about 1400. Once again the Japanese were watching. The submarine *I-19* put three torpedoes into the carrier, and even though Capt. Forrest Sherman did everything possible to avert the disaster he could not avoid the "fish."

This was no joke, this torpedoing. The carrier erupted in flame and smoke as the explosions smashed her. The gasoline in the tanks spread through the ship and caught fire, sending licking tongues of flame everywhere. The water mains broke down forward, making it almost impossible to fight the fires. Captain Sherman still had communications within the ship, and control, but for how long?

In half an hour the ship was a mass of flame, and one explosion very nearly did for Rear Adm. Leigh Noyes, the task force commander. Another submarine, *I-15*, tried to torpedo *Hornet*, which was not far away, and did manage to put one torpedo into the battleship *North Carolina* and another into the destroyer *O'Brien*, but *Hornet* escaped.

On *Wasp* Captain Sherman was still trying to fight the fires. He moved away from the bridge, which had become untenable. Then an explosion threw the No. 2 flight elevator high into the air, and fires spread further. Captain Sherman and Admiral Noyes conferred and agreed that the fires were out of control. The order to abandon ship was given at 1520.

The process of evacuation was orderly enough, and went on until 1600 when Captain Sherman left the ship. Of the 2,247 men aboard, 193 were killed and 366 wounded. All but one of the twenty-five planes aloft were saved by *Hornet*, but here was another carrier out of action.

So now the South Pacific air force consisted of the planes at Henderson Field, a growing force around Espiritu Santu, and Task Force 17, commanded by Rear Adm. George Murray, centered around *Hornet*. This carrier force was used carefully. In one October day her planes raided Rekata Bay, Santa Isabel, and destroyed a dozen Japanese seaplanes in the water. The planes also attacked the Japanese on Guadalcanal. But caution was the word—until Halsey returned to take over command of the South Pacific force, and *Enterprise* returned to help fight the battle.

Enterprise had a new Air Group, Air Group 10, but John Crommelin was still the air officer. She was ready to fight again, and so now were the Japanese. In mid-October they committed four carriers and many other ships to the battle to reconquer Guadalcanal. *Shokaku* and *Zuikaku* were out, and so were *Zuiho* and *Junyo*, another dangerous pair.

On October 25 American scouting planes found the Japanese and identified two carriers; although a strike went out, it was too late and the pilots missed the enemy that day. But the next day Commander Crommelin's boys were ready. Out in the morning, the scouting force from *Enterprise* found the enemy just before eight o'clock. Lt. Birney Strong and Ens. Charles Irvine were not far away, flying planes that each carried a 500-pound bomb. They headed for the position, and at 0830 Strong spotted *Shokaku* and *Zuiho* beneath them. Dared two planes attack these carriers alone? Strong said yes, and charged his guns. They moved into the sun so the enemy would not easily see them—and no one did. The carriers below were strangely quiet, the ships around them did not shoot; there were no Zeros to intercept.

They dived, heading for *Zuiho*, the nearest carrier. Irvine was following Strong, 1,000 feet behind. Down they went to

1,500 feet, and then released. The bombs fell away. Then the antiaircraft began to come up, and Zeros popped out from all corners of the convoy. But the enemy had given Strong and Irvine that most wonderful of all opportunities for the dive-bomber pilot, a clear and unobstructed easy shot—and both took advantage of it as they were trained to do. Both 500-bombs went into *Zuiho*'s flight deck and blew up.

Zuiho was lucky that day: all her planes had taken off to strike the Americans, and so although the bombs hurt the ship, they did not sink her. Had the planes been aboard, fires might have started and put an end to this carrier as flames had destroyed the carriers at Midway.

Strong and Irvine hurried back to *Enterprise* and landed, almost out of fuel—indeed Strong would not have had enough gas for making a second pass if he had been ordered to go around.

Now *Enterprise* and *Hornet* were launching their strikes against the Japanese force; the Japanese had already put their planes in the air and were heading toward the American carriers, which had run into trouble. The torpedo bombers were jumped by a force of Zeros on their way to the target, and several bombers were shot down. The F4Fs were down low, escorting the bombers, and the Zeros got the jump on them.

One fighter pilot on this mission was Ens. Dusty Rhodes, who suddenly found a Zero on his tail. He tried to drop his extra fuel tank, but it would not release; worse, a Zero set it afire. He looped and turned and dove down on the deck and tried to escape the tank and the Zeros. Finally the fire burned itself out as the gasoline left the tank, and he was able to fight again, although slowed by the extra drag. His radio was shot to pieces, and so was his instrument panel. He and another pilot flew a defensive pattern, trying to get back to their carrier, but the faster Zeros were after them all the time, and the air seemed to be full of them. Finally, Rhodes's engine burned out, and he started to ditch. Another Zero came after him and shot away his rudder controls. He was too low to bail out, under 500 feet, but he ripped back the canopy, and stood up in the cockpit, pulled the ripcord, and let the chute pull him out of the plane. The plane shot out from under him, the chute snapped open and pulled him up—and then he hit the water. He went deep, but he came up and disengaged himself from the chute. He saw the planes headed south, three Zeros after one F4F. Dusty Rhodes sat in his life raft and waved at American planes as they came over, hoping someone would see him.

The strikes from *Enterprise* and *Hornet* went on. *Hornet*'s bombers found *Shokaku* and smashed her with several 1,000-pound bombs. They came in at 0930, fifteen of them, and *Shokaku* seemed to explode beneath them. She took four 1,000-pounders on the port side of the flight deck. But this fleet carrier was tough, and the fires and damage were brought under control. She survived, to go home for repairs. She would be out of action for nine months, but she was still alive.

Zuikaku and *Junyo* were also alive, and they were untouched and launching planes to hit the Americans. They came in, these Japanese, and they missed *Enterprise*, which was in the shadow of a rain squall at the time. They did not miss *Hornet*, but headed for her with their deadly bombs and torpedoes.

The fighters of *Hornet* and *Enterprise* clustered around, even chasing the Japanese into the antiaircraft fire from the American ships. But the Japanese were courageous and skillful and they had an advantage: most of the American planes were not here to cover the carriers. The Japanese put everything they had into the attack. One bomb hit and then another. The Japanese squadron commander, his plane damaged, dove into the carrier carrying his bomb. His plane hit the stack and bounced down through the flight deck as two bombs exploded. And then in came the "Kates," the torpedo planes. Two torpedoes exploded in the engine rooms, and the carrier began to shoot up a cloud of smoke. Three more big bombs hit the flight deck and destroyed the ship's communications. Then a doomed Kate came flaming in and blew up near the forward elevator shaft. The Japanese had attacked with twenty-seven planes: twenty-five of them were lost, but they had smashed the *Hornet*. Every effort was made to save her, including bucket brigades when the water failed, but it was a losing battle.

Meanwhile, *Enterprise* was hurt again this day. Standing on the bridge, Commander Crommelin watched a wave of Japanese planes come in. He looked at one in particular. "I think that son of a bitch is going to get us," he said casually. And just then a 550-pound bomb ripped through the overhang of the flight deck. A moment later another bomb hit the middle of the flight deck and broke in half: one half destroyed two planes; the other went through the deck and killed many men. Bomb after bomb fell near, showering the carrier with spray and knocking men out of position at the guns. At 1119 came a terrible explosion aft of the island, and it sounded as though the ship was done for. But the sky was clear of Japanese planes, and it seemed to be over. Yet not quite. In half an hour a flight of fifteen torpedo planes came boring in. Three planes made perfect drops, and the torpedoes came in, their wakes sizzling. On the bridge, the captain turned the ship hard right and missed them by ten yards, running at forty knots. Another torpedo came in on the starboard bow, and the captain kicked the ship around to port. There were five more torpedo attacks, and then it really was over. In spite of the damage, *Enterprise* got into position and began taking aboard her planes. Out in the ocean, Ensign Rhodes sat in his swamped life raft until dusk, when a destroyer picked him up. Unfortunately it was a Japanese destroyer.

But he was luckier than many of *Hornet*'s men, who died on their blazing carrier that day. Attempts were made to save her, but they were hampered by the Japanese attacks. More planes came in to hit *Hornet*. She was finally abandoned, and that night was destroyed by Japanese torpedoes. So ended the battle called the Battle of Santa Cruz, which was undoubtedly a Japanese victory. It left the Americans with only one carrier in the area. But the only big Japanese carrier left now was *Zuikaku*, and as they lost ships they could not easily replace the Japanese became more conservative. They did not press their victory and so lost the fruits of it. Admiral Nagumo, in *Shokaku*, had once again the frightful experience of seeing his ship in flames around him, although this time it was saved.

Thus the carriers did not play a vital role in the rest of the South Pacific campaign, except to destroy the Japanese battleship *Hiei*. The carrier's planes, sometimes flying from Henderson Field, joined land-based air-power in helping to smash the Japanese, but this was not the prime purpose of carriers. *Enterprise* went back to Pearl in the spring of 1943, and then became a part of something new in carrier warfare.

CHAPTER SIX

The Fast Carriers

By the summer of 1943 the whole concept of the carrier war had changed, and the United States was far ahead of any other nation in developing this new warfare. The carriers themselves had changed, drastically. There was the new *Essex* class, a 27,100-ton ship that might carry 3,100 officers and men, and more fighters and bombers than the old carriers. Another type was the light carrier of the *Independence* class, an 11,000-ton ship that carried about 1,600 officers and men, and far fewer planes. Still another was the escort carrier, a "baby flattop" built on a merchantship hull; for the most part this was used for escort and antisubmarine patrol.

The new carriers were vast improvements over the old, which were modernized as much as possible that year. The new carriers' focal points of activity were the captain's bridge, forward on the island, and the admiral's bridge (if there was an admiral aboard) one level below. This bridge was also used by the air officer to direct flight operations, so it was never waste space. Next to this bridge were gunnery control, the photo laboratory, and radio air plot, all vital to the swift function of a carrier force. Air plot controlled the pilots in their planes, feeding them the information—even as it changed—necessary to get to the target and to get home. Down below, one deck beneath the flight deck, was the combat information center, a maze of wires and men speaking into microphones, which collated and disseminated all the information about an action as it progressed.

Radar was the key to the success of the carriers. The acronym stood for Radio Detection and Ranging, and with it the operator could track ships and planes by means of the little blips that appeared on the radar screen. To separate friendly planes from enemy ones, the ship also had an IFF system, or Identification-Friend-or-Foe, by which a plane sent out a signal that identified it to the carrier force and kept Americans from shooting down other Americans (except when pilots forgot to turn on their IFF button).

Radio had become so advanced that fighter directors could send their attack units out with ease, and at the same time a half dozen other functions could be carried out.

For defense the new carriers had five-inch guns, 40-mm. Bofors guns, and 20-mm. Oerlikon guns. They also had the proximity fuse, which meant that an antiaircraft gunner did not actually have to strike the incoming enemy plane to damage it; his shell would explode close enough to do the job. The big *Essex* class carriers had seventeen sets of 40-mm. guns mounted in four-barrel units and sixty-five single-mount 20-mm. guns. The *Independence* class CVLs, or light carriers, had two sets of 40-mm. four-barrel mounts, and nine twin-mounted 20-mm. guns. The big carriers had six five-inch guns, which could fire a shell ten miles, firing twelve to fifteen rounds per minute, shooting those proximity-fused shells that would explode thirty or forty feet away from an incoming plane.

The *Essex* class carriers mounted a formidable fighting force, which had now been trained very well indeed. The Japanese suffered after Coral Sea and Midway because they had never rotated their airmen; a pilot was assigned to an air group and the group to a carrier until he or the carrier died. But the Americans had been sending pilots back to be instructors since the early days of the war, and this rotating experience and training was paying off.

No longer was the Japanese Zero the finest fighter in the air. The Americans now had the F6F Hellcat, a plane with a 2,000-horsepower engine that could fly thirty miles an hour faster than the Zero and climb 2,000 feet higher, both climbing and diving better than the Japanese plane. It also carried six fifty-caliber machine guns that fired 1,000 rounds a minute, and experiments were being carried out with 20-mm.

cannon and rockets. Each big carrier would have thirty-six of these fighters.

The big carriers would also have thirty-six bombers, used for scouting and as dive-bombers. The new SB2C Helldivers were coming in to replace the old SBDs. And, after Midway, the American fleet got a new torpedo bomber, the TBF-1 Avenger, and even more improved types. A big carrier would have thirty-six dive-bombers and eighteen torpedo bombers. A small carrier would have twenty-four fighters and nine torpedo bombers.

By the summer of 1943 the American shipbuilding program, and the emphasis on carriers, was beginning to pay off. The *Essex* came to Pearl Harbor and was joined by the new *Yorktown*, which replaced the carrier lost at Midway. Then came a new *Lexington* and the light carriers *Independence, Princeton,* and *Belleau Wood.* They were joined by the CV or fleet carrier *Bunker Hill,* light carriers *Cowpens* and *Monterey,* and no fewer than eight escort carriers that mounted sixteen fighters and twelve torpedo bombers.

Yorktown was commanded by Capt. J.J. Clark, an aggressive aviation officer who would make a reputation as one of the carrier admirals who were coming up as this form of warfare developed. Clark had already made some reputation for himself in command of the escort carrier *Swannee* in the Atlantic. Now he was to have his chance with the "big boys" and with the new planes, the F6Fs, the Curtiss Helldiver SB2Cs and the TBF Avengers. But he did not like the Helldivers, so Captain Clark managed to get a change to SBD dive-bombers, which were slower but more dependable.

After some time at Pearl Harbor, *Yorktown* set out on August 23, 1943, along with *Essex, Independence,* and several lesser ships plus one battleship, for a raid against Marcus Island. The unit was called Task Force 15, and its purpose was to see what the new fast carriers could do. It had been shown in the South Pacific that individual carrier force operation was not very successful—the Japanese had operated with carriers in groups, and they had certainly won at Santa Cruz. Now, with the American shipyards going at full blast, the United States Navy in the Pacific was getting the fast carriers it needed, and the tactics of carrier operation as presented by the new young admirals were to be tested.

Commander of this group was Rear Adm. C.A. Pownall, and another carrier admiral, Rear Adm. A.E. Montgomery, came along for the ride.

The operation began on August 31, when the carrier reached a point 130 miles northeast of Marcus. The planes launched in the dark; this was one of the new techniques, and at 0422 the flight was getting into the air. At 0605 the planes were hitting Marcus and strafing the airfield there. They stayed on the target all day, the planes shuttling back and forth to the carrier for gas and rearming. Another new technique was the sign of the confidence of the navy and the number of ships available in 1943: a submarine was assigned to the task force for rescue purposes.

The operation was a success. The fast carriers gave the pilots a good deal more confidence than they had in the past, and the new planes were superior to the Japanese fighters and bombers. For the first time the navy fliers would have equipment that would give them a break.

The next test was more extensive: an attack on Wake Island. Admiral Montgomery was in charge of the operation, and he was teaching Rear Adm. Arthur Radford and Rear Adm. Van H. Ragsdale the tricks of the trade. So they went out, *Essex* and *Yorktown, Lexington* and *Cowpens, Independence* and *Belleau Wood*—six carriers working together, mounting 375 planes.

This time the carriers had air opposition. The Japanese put up thirty-three fighters, and the F6Fs were eager to take them on. How times had changed! This time the Americans shot down twenty-seven Japanese fighters, losing only three of their own. There were two reasons for the disparity. One was the equipment: for the first time the Americans had the superior plane, and they would not lose that advantage during the rest of the war. Also, the American pilots were better trained, for Japan had suffered terrible manpower losses in the South Pacific campaign as well as carrier plane losses, and she was not keeping up with the demand in her training program.

The Wake operation gave the new breed of carrier admirals and carrier captains an entirely different outlook on the war from the one the old carrier captains had. Captain Clark and his peers could see what a powerful weapon they possessed, and they were determined to use it to the best of their ability. Clark was called Jocko, and he lived up to one definition of the name by his daring and flamboyant method of jockeying a 27,000-ton carrier around the Pacific. One day when operating under Admiral Pownall, who was on board the carrier, Clark brought *Essex* around at high speed, slid in between a half dozen lesser ships, and smacked the carrier into formation, like a hot-rod youngster jockeying a sixteen-foot speedboat. Pownall was aghast, and made Clark promise not to do it again—at least while he was aboard. But Clark had a fine sense of what he was doing; he knew how the *Yorktown* would behave, and he wanted to make use of every bit of her ability.

In two days of hanging around Wake (which earlier carrier groups would not have done for fear of reprisal) the task force flew 1,100 sorties against the Japanese, and at the end reduced the opposition to only sporadic antiaircraft fire. Their planes shot down sixty-five Japanese planes, either in the air or on the ground, until there was nothing coming up against them. They destroyed the only ship in harbor, a tanker, and blew up all the noticeable installations. They lost twelve planes in combat, but the submarine picked up six fliers; they lost another fourteen planes in what they called "operational mishaps"—deck crashes and failures that sent planes into the sea. Overall, it was a highly satisfactory operation.

But now, back at Pearl Harbor, erupted the simmering dispute between battleship men and carrier men. The coming of the fast carriers in huge numbers had changed the whole nature of the war—or could do so. The carrier men wanted to go out and smash the enemy in his bases; the battleship men wanted to use the carriers as a part of the fleet, to put up an air umbrella during the offensive operations.

Admiral Nimitz resolved the matter by his usual shrewd sense of compromise. The carriers would be given a good deal of freedom, and would go after Japanese bases. But in offensive operations against Japanese bases where the object was to seize territory, the carriers would provide the umbrella for the invasion fleet. The solution did not satisfy Jocko Clark and his other hard-driving young captains and admirals, who claimed the war could be shortened immeasurably by waging it their way, but it did bring the carriers into effective play as a new kind of offensive weapon.

Now at Pearl Harbor Admiral Nimitz and Admiral Spruance were planning the first big move across the central Pacific, the invasion of the Gilbert Islands. After two years of starvation rations in ships and materiel, the Pacific command was beginning to get more attention from the logistic wizards in Washington. Spruance would have a fleet, to be called the Fifth Fleet, and its nuclei would be the new fast battleships that were coming off the ways, the new fast carrier force, and the many cruisers and destroyers would support them. In addition to the six carriers that fought at Wake, in came *Bunker Hill*, a new carrier, *Saratoga* and *Enterprise*, and the new light carrier *Monterey*. As this force began to assemble it was hard to remember that just a year before the Americans had been strained to put three carriers into the Pacific to fight down around Guadalcanal.

As the plans were made, there were conflicts. Square, ruddy-faced Jocko Clark, part Cherokee Indian and a fighter all the way, spoke his mind loudly around Pearl Harbor about the shortsightedness of the "black-shoe boys" who wanted to use carriers as support ships. The aviation officers were "brown shoes"—the distinction stemmed from the dress regulation that permitted aviation officers to wear brown shoes with their flight uniforms. But with Spruance in command, and his very careful measurement of opportunity and risk, it was certain that the carriers would be used to support the fleet.

A remarkable array of carriers set forth to assault the Gilbert Islands and secure for the United States a new jumping-off point in the Pacific. Six escort carriers were assigned to support the Marines directly. Task Force 50, which the new fast carrier force was now named, included six fleet carriers and five light carriers, divided into four task groups, each with a rear admiral in command. Admiral Pownall was in command of Task Group 50.1, which included Jocko Clark's *Yorktown, Lexington,* and *Cowpens,* with Pownall riding with Clark in *Yorktown.*

The job of Task Group 50.1 at the Gilberts invasion was to guard a sector of the sea and air from the Japanese. The air admirals argued that the best thing to do was send the fast carriers in against the Marshalls, and destroy Japanese air strength right there. Admiral Nimitz disagreed—the Japanese had a pipeline of land bases around the Empire. They could send planes from Japan on hops from island to island, and to the Marshalls again. So if the carriers hit the Marshalls and destroyed the planes, the Japanese could still reinforce the Marshalls and send planes to attack the American fleet.

The Gilbert and Marshall Islands lie close together, and *Yorktown*'s job was to patrol north of Makin Island in the Gilberts (which would be attacked along with Tarawa), and to attack Jaluit and Mili Islands in the southern Marshalls to keep planes from their fields away from the landings. On November 18, Jocko Clark had his ship on station, and for the next five days her planes did that job. The fast carrier men were still learning—Clark was adamant that every bogey that appeared on the radar screen had to be checked out, and as flagship for the task group *Yorktown* sent her planes to do the checking. There was a new element, too, in the Japanese night attack, which the fast carriers had not yet learned about. They learned this trip, when a Japanese force of twenty bombers put a torpedo into the carrier *Independence* and put her out of action for several months. The fast carrier men had to learn how to handle their ships against this new menace. One night Admiral Pownall stopped all the carriers so the Japanese night attackers could not see the wakes of the ships. The plan worked very well, but it frightened Clark and the other fast carrier advocates because they felt helpless—they believed in speed and maneuverability, and not staying in one place long enough for the enemy to figure out where they would operate. They lamented the idea of a fixed area of operations, and Clark said openly that that was what had caused the disabling of *Saratoga* and *Enterprise* and the sinking of *Wasp* and *Hornet* in the South Pacific. The carrier should be a hit-and-run weapon, and so should the carrier task force.

Jocko Clark nearly lost his carrier on this operation. On the evening of November 23, when a storm came up, five planes from the escort carrier *Liscome Bay* appeared over *Yorktown* and asked to be taken on. Clark and Pownall agreed and the planes began to land. The first pair did all right, but the third plane bounced when it hit the deck, and since the pilot had forgotten to lower his tail hook there was nothing to catch the arresting cable. The pilot thought he would take off and come around again and gunned his engine. The plane jumped and bounced again, this time over the wire barrier that protected parked planes from the landing area. The belly tank exploded and set fire to ammunition and flares stored in the area. The pilot of the plane squirmed free as the flames roared up, and the damage control parties rushed forward with foam extinguishers to smother the fire as the air officer on the bridge ordered the other two planes to land on *Lexington*.

It was as bad as if they had taken a Japanese fragmentation bomb—the fire was burning fiercely on the deck, five men had already been killed in the explosion, and Clark managed to keep the planes parked forward from blazing up only by steaming fast into the wind to keep the fire burning aft.

As the fire burned, the heat drifted back and up to the island, until the men on the bridge could barely stand it. There was very definite danger that the island would catch fire, until a man in an asbestos suit came out and began playing a hose to keep the fire back. Gasoline spilled down into the hangar deck and burned, and for a time some feared for the carrier. But fourteen minutes later the fire was under control. Hours later the five bodies could be moved from the smoldering wreckage and the five destroyed planes pushed over the side. Cleanup crews worked that night, and by morning the only signs of the disaster were a few scorches on the flight deck— an apt illustration of the recuperative powers of carrier and crew.

Yorktown was luckier than Clark knew that night. The Japanese had sent out nine submarines to attack the American ships in the Gilberts, and the fire on *Yorktown*'s deck made her a prime target. But apparently no Japanese were looking. That night, ironically enough, the Japanese sank *Liscome Bay*, from which the offending carrier plane had originated, but they did not bother *Yorktown*. The sinking of this escort carrier was a real tragedy. She went down fast and took with her fifty-one officers and five hundred ninety-one men, plus the captain of the ship and the admiral in command of the escort carriers, Rear Adm. Henry Mullinix. One trouble with a carrier was that its cargo of airplanes, ammunition, and high octane gas made it very vulnerable and very dangerous when attacked.

By dawn on November 24, *Yorktown* was back in business launching planes to hit the southern Marshalls, but the action was nearly over. Jocko Clark still felt strongly about the confinement of the carriers to sectors of the sea, saying this tactic left them sitting ducks for attack. On the night of November 27 his charge seemed justified. The Japanese came in with another of their night air attacks, against Admiral Radford's group. The fighters went up and drove them off, but lost several planes. It was the contention of the carrier admirals that the loss was unnecessary, caused by keeping the carriers cooped up.

For weeks Jocko Clark and other commanders had been asking for permission to hit Kwajalein, the big Japanese air base in the Marshalls, not far from where they were. They received permission, and two task groups moved up there, expecting heavy fighter opposition because this base had given a lot of trouble. They steamed north, and on December 4 *Yorktown* began putting her planes up early in the morning. They found a treasure trove for a fighting carrier admiral: some thirty ships in harbor, including two light cruisers, a score of seaplanes moored in shallow waters, and then sixty torpedo bombers parked on the airfield at Roi. Out of the sky came some fifty Zeros to mix it up with the fighters and give them a very rough time, shooting down several (although the Americans downed eighteen Japanese fighters and ten bombers).

Jocko Clark learned about the bombers on the airstrip, and

agreed with his excited pilots who came up on the bridge to tell him that they ought to go back and "smack" them. But on his admiral's bridge, "Baldy" Pownall had the old admiral's worry: they were hanging around the fringes of a Japanese strong point, and he had the feeling they had already been there too long. He ordered the task group to turn around and go home; they had accomplished their mission, he said, which was primarily to take pictures of Kwajalein for intelligence. Clark argued. They ought to knock out those Japanese bombers, he said, because if they did not they would have to take the consequences when the fleet came back to take the Marshalls, which was the next scheduled operation in the Central Pacific.

No, said Pownall. And since he was in command, that was it.

That very day the task group felt some of the consequences of the failure to hit the airfield. Those Japanese planes came in force and attacked *Lexington*, which barely dodged one torpedo, and another very nearly got *Yorktown*.

They moved out in a hurry then, recovering their planes and then heading north at twenty-five knots. But they were still within range of the Japanese land-based planes of the Micronesian Islands, and these planes attacked, dropping flares over the American ships. In the earlier attack at night, Admiral Radford's night fighters from *Enterprise* had broken up the enemy game, with the loss of the legendary hero Butch O'Hare. Now they had no O'Hare, nor did the task group have any pilots trained in the special techniques needed for effective night interception. When some fifty Japanese planes were boring in, there was some regret about that lack.

Jocko Clark's men fought back valiantly, particularly the 20-mm. and 40-mm. antiaircraft gunners. Two torpedoes passed by the ship very close, but they did not hit.

Her sister ship *Lexington* was not so lucky, and at 2300 she was struck by a torpedo that exploded under her stern and jammed her rudder. Then the task group had to stand by and fight off other Japanese planes until repairs were made before heading back for the safety of Pearl Harbor.

Back at Pearl, the operation was surveyed from the point of

view of learning from mistakes. This had been the first use of the fast carriers with the fleet to support a landing operation. Admiral Nimitz had known there would be mistakes, and now he studied them. One of the mistakes, obviously, was the use made of the fast carriers, and Clark went to complain about it. He found Forrest Sherman, late of the *Wasp*, now an admiral and planning officer for Nimitz. He showed him the pictures of the bombers left sitting on Roi airstrip and told his story. Sherman called in Adm. "Soc" McMorris and other officers, and they marveled over the pictures—"The fish that got away."

Actually, the staff at Pearl Harbor was ahead of Jocko Clark in this, or right with him. The reason the carriers had been released toward the end of the Gilberts operation was that Adm. Jack Towers, the air commander in the Pacific, had argued as Clark did, that to leave the carriers in a single area was to endanger them. Spruance had objected to being deprived of his carrier support, even toward the end of the operation, but Nimitz had overruled him.

Changes were in the wind. Nimitz saw that he needed a highly experienced aviator and carrier man to take over the big fast carrier task force, and he settled on Rear Adm. Marc A. Mitscher, who had been a mere captain in command of *Hornet* during Doolittle's Tokyo Raid. But Mitscher was everything a carrier man could respect, an aviator through and through, a pilot who had flown every kind of craft himself and knew the difficulties inside out, and a great fighting man in the Halsey tradition. With his arrival, the fast carrier task force came of age.

CHAPTER SEVEN

Enter Mitscher

Admiral Mitscher came to Pearl Harbor early in January, just in time to stop what was becoming an unseemly row between Spruance and Admiral Towers over the employment of the fast carriers during the coming invasion of the Marshalls. All this argument was occurring during the absence of Admiral Nimitz, who was on the mainland conferring with Admiral King. It might not have come to much if Nimitz had been there, because Nimitz had been quick to realize the strengths of the new carrier weapon and to act to relieve them of tedious and dangerous routine. But at any rate Mitscher's coming was like a breath of fresh air to the carrier men, who wanted someone *who knew* and someone who would lead them into glorious battle.

His chief recommendation to Nimitz had been the aggressive way in which he had chewed up the Japanese land-based air-power in the last few months under Halsey's command in the South Pacific. And now he was ready to undertake a new adventure. He was wizened, scarcely recovered from the malaria that had dropped him down to 115 pounds during the Guadalcanal months. But he was ready to fight and eager to see what could be done with this new command. He was also ready to give these young eager admirals and captains their heads, if they could perform. "I tell them what I want done, not how," he said.

Mitscher came in and hoisted his flag in *Yorktown,* Jocko Clark's ship. He had an empire all his own in the ship, which controlled the whole task force. The center of it was the room in the island called flag plot, which was the communications control for all. The most prominent piece of furniture was a big chart table, and around the bulkheads were radar screens that showed the positions of ships and aircraft. Various boards showed the status of ships and location and the same of planes. There was a multitude of communications and special equipment, and a long brown leather couch on which Mitscher spent most of his time, unless he was on the flag bridge watching, or in his little sea cabin aft of flag plot. Down below in the vastness of the carrier's bulk, he had a much more elaborate cabin for use when he felt the need or the luxury of it. But most of the time he was in flag plot, a crowded and busy place usually occupied by perhaps twenty people, talking and moving about at their tasks, while other officers scurried up and down from the combat information center or the intelligence center, watching the wizened little man on the couch, or sitting out in his swivel chair on the wing of the bridge.

Mitscher came aboard for the Marshalls invasion on January 13, carrying a detective story, and ready to go. He was a little uneasy about the future, because he knew his head could roll as quickly as had Baldy Pownall's—and the fact that Pownall was a favorite of Admiral Spruance, that Pownall and Spruance shared ideas about the way carriers should be operated—did not help a bit. Mitscher did not at all agree with Spruance's conservative carrier technique. He was an airman through and through, and as they approached the Marshalls for the operation the two disagreed in signals several times. It was Spruance's show, and his will would prevail, but Mitscher was going to do everything he could to make the carriers useful as *fighting* weapons, not for defense of the battleships.

The work began on January 29, D-Day minus two for the invasion. At 0500 the warmup of the planes began. Soon they were in the air, 700 of them. The Japanese had only 150 planes in the Marshalls to defend, and although the Americans did not know it the Japanese high command had already decided to call the garrisons of the islands expendable. The Japanese would fight and fight hard, but the high command

The U.S.S. *Enterprise*, as seen from an SBD
(scout bomber) which has just taken off. The U.S.S.
Lexington can be seen in the background (right). July 1944.

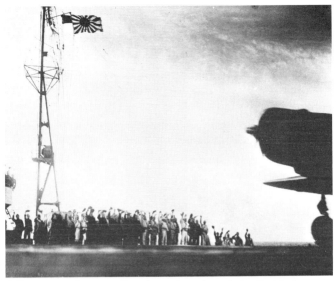

A Japanese photograph taken aboard a carrier just before the attack on Pearl Harbor.

A captured Japanese photograph taken during the attack on Pearl Harbor. December 7, 1941.

Takeoff, from the deck of the U.S.S. *Hornet*, of an Army
B-25 on its way to take part in the first U.S. air raid on
Japan. April 1942.

Navy SBDs during the attack on the Japanese fleet off
Midway, June 4-6, 1942. In the center, a burning Japanese
ship is visible.

The 19,900-ton U.S.S. *Yorktown* lists heavily to the port side after attack by Japanese bombers and torpedo planes in the Battle of Midway, June 4, 1942. The aircraft carrier was struck by two torpedoes launched by an enemy submarine on June 6, and capsized and sank the following day. A destroyer (right) was taken almost dead astern of the *Yorktown*.

The U.S.S. *Lexington* burns following the Battle of Coral Sea. May 8, 1942.

Aerial view of the launching of the carrier U.S.S. *Yorktown*. January 21, 1943.

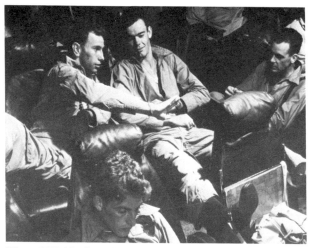

These VF-16 pilots, in the ready room of the U.S.S. *Lexington*, have seen recent action in the Marshall Islands attack. November 23, 1943.

Navy dive-bomber pilots report to the Air Combat Information officer aboard their carrier after a strike against the Japanese on Wake Island. The attack was carried out by a Pacific Fleet task force on October 5 and 6 and resulted in the destruction of enemy planes, together with shipping, supply depots, and airfield installations.

Damage control. October 1943.

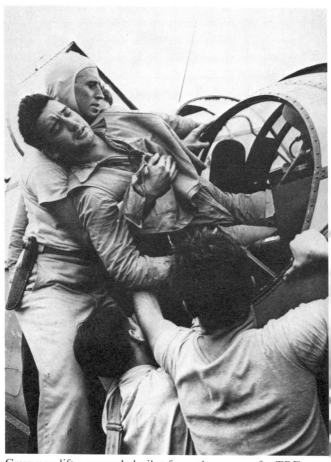

Crewmen lift a wounded pilot from the turret of a TBF on the U.S.S. *Saratoga* after the raid on Rabaul. November 1943.

A Navy TBF-1c Grumman "Avenger" with rockets under its wings, part of Air Squadron VC-7, on the first Marshall Islands invasion. This photograph was taken by plane from the U.S.S. *Manila Bay* over Kwajalein. February 4, 1944.

Firing practice aboard the U.S.S. *Altamaha*—it takes teamwork to handle those 40mm guns. August 1944.

Pilot of Air Squadron VF-16, aboard the U.S.S. *Lexington*, during the attack on Saipan in the Marianas. His total is now nineteen Japanese planes. June 19, 1944.

The Navy buries its dead at sea from the U.S.S. *Lexington* after being attacked by a Japanese crash-diving plane. November 6, 1944.

CV-3 U.S.S. *Saratoga* hit by a kamikaze off Iwo Jima.
February 21, 1945.

A typhoon-damaged aircraft is salvaged aboard the U.S.S. *Altamaha.* December 1944.

-38s are spotted on the flight deck of the U.S.S. *Ranger* in
ymmetrical rows ready for transport to an advanced allied
ase. Plastiphane covering is used for weatherproofing
lanes. April 23, 1944.

. Japanese "ZEKE" making a run on the U.S.S. *Essex*. It
as shot down by alert ship gunners somewhere in the
acific. May 14, 1945.

Japanese CVL ZUIHO under attack by the U.S.S. *Enterprise* Air Group 20 in the Philippine Sea. This very low aerial photograph was taken from the torpedo plane a few seconds before the torpedo hit aft on the starboard side, helping to sink her. Task Groups 38.2, 38.3, and 38.4 participated in this engagement. Note camouflage design on the flight deck. October 25, 1944.

On the flight deck of the U.S.S. *Belleau Wood*, crewmen fight a roaring fire, which resulted from a kamikaze attack. October 30, 1944.

The U.S.S. *Bunker Hill* at sea. October 16, 1945.

Recreation on Majuro Atoll, Marshall Islands. May 14, 1946.

would not send the fleet or the carriers or the reinforcements that it might have done.

By noon on the first day Mitscher's boys had secured air control over the region, and they did not lose it. By the end of the day not one enemy plane remained operational east of Eniwetok. They got all those planes parked on Roi this time.

Next day the planes roared over Eniwetok and other islands in the area, doing what came to be known in the force as the "Mitscher shampoo," which preceded the "Spruance haircut" that left palm trees looking like matchsticks once the big ships had stopped their bombardment.

That was about all there was to the Marshalls operation. As far as Japanese air opposition was concerned, for the most part it had been wiped out in the Gilberts move earlier. The Japanese lost a total of 155 planes, and the American task force lost 57. The pattern was set for the future. Mitscher would be in command of the fast carriers.

A much more important test of the carriers came a little later in the year. For a long time Admiral Nimitz had been eager to knock out the important Japanese naval base at Truk, in the Micronesian Islands. Since the beginning of the war Truk had been important. During the South Pacific campaign all kinds of hell for the Marines and navy had originated in Truk, and now, with this fast carrier force available between major landing operations, Nimitz wanted to eliminate the base if he could as an important Japanese focal point.

Actually, the Americans were coming a bit late. On February 10 the Japanese naval force evacuated Truk, which the high command considered to be unusable now that the Gilberts and Marshalls had fallen. But Nimitz did not know that. On February 3 aerial observation had shown the masts of some twenty naval vessels poking through a cloud over the island, and it was this information that the fleet would follow. On February 12, two days after the fleet left Truk, the Americans sailed from Majuro. Three task groups were to hit the base. Mitscher had a lot of ideas that he wanted to try out. One was for close maneuvering of the carriers, an idea that frightened some ship captains. But if the ship captains could not handle their ships, said the admiral, then they had better get off at Pearl and give command to someone who could. And he liked to hide under a storm front, then come out and make his attack, thus always able to duck back into squalls (as had *Zuikaku* that day of the battle of Santa Cruz) and avoid enemy counterattacks. He also always wanted an initial fighter sweep over a target before the bombers came—this way the target area was cleared of enemy planes that might harry the slower bombers.

And then there were other little tricks, like directing the last bombers of the day over an area to drop 1,000-pound bombs on the airfield runways so they could not be repaired easily that night. And to save strikes on fuel dumps until the last, so the smoke and flame would not rise up and inhibit the hitting of other targets.

All these tricks would be tried at Truk. When the ships were on their way and the admiral announced their destination, some of the pilots felt like jumping overboard. Truk had been known since 1941 as the danger of dangers, in the heart of Japanese country. But the target was Truk.

The attack began at 0600 on February 16. On the carriers pilots and crewmen filed into the ready rooms and settled down for their briefing. The force was about 100 miles northeast of Truk, with rain clouds around—just the condition Mitscher liked.

On the flight decks the wings of the fighters were unfolded and the planes began moving into position. In true Mitscher style the first wave would be a fighter sweep, and in fifteen minutes they began going up off the decks of the carriers and heading for the dreaded base.

One reason Truk was so badly dreaded was that no one had dared fly over it before, until that Marine B-24 reconnaissance plane had gone in bad weather within the fortnight. What the planes found was a great circling coral reef, thirty miles in diameter, and within that the celebrated anchorage, the Truk lagoon. For years the Japanese had guarded the secrets of Truk; now they were about to be unveiled.

The fighters swept in to see a dozen volcanic islands in the lagoon, providing good anchoring, and indicating the depth and comfort of the harbor. As they moved in across the blue water some fifty Japanese fighters came up to meet them, fifty assorted Japanese fighters against seventy-four F6Fs that could outfly and outfight them all. And then the tangle began, for the Japanese were growing tougher as the Americans moved into their territory, and these pilots on Truk were the remnants of the old highly trained Japanese of three years before.

The sky was a maze of brown Japanese fighters with the red balls of the rising sun on their wings and tails, and blue Hellcats with their American insignia. Planes spun crazily to the ground and to the sea, and in the harbor the ships opened up with their antiaircraft guns. The fast Hellcats were all around their enemies, hitting here and there, catching planes trying to take off from the airfields and shooting them down before they could get truly airborne. They twisted and turned and chased the little planes, fired and fired again, dodged and sent their tracers into the brown fuselages. The air was filled with screaming engines and the swish of the diving, the rattle of machine guns punctuated by the coughing of the Japanese cannon and the bark of antiaircraft guns.

In an hour it was just about over, completely over in an hour and a half. The Americans had lost four fighters, and for that they had shot down thirty planes and destroyed another forty on the ground. No more Japanese came up to meet them as they circled and strafed any targets that seemed likely.

It was only 0930 when Mitscher's bombers came in, just as he had planned, to clear skies and very little trouble, to do their work in leisurely efficiency. Some of the planes carried fragmentation bombs in 100-pound clusters and incendiaries also in clusters. They went after the service installations on the air fields. Then came the dive-bombers with the 1,000-pound bombs, moving in to hit the ships at Dublon anchorage. There was not much there by the standards of two weeks before—the fleet was gone for the most part, but there were some merchantmen and a pair of cruisers. The bombers hit a merchantman and made a near miss on a cruiser in the first pass. More fighters came in with the bombers, and their job was to strafe the antiaircraft guns that were still popping at the planes. The bombers came back again and again, set the tanker aflame, hit a little carrier they found tucked away at anchor, and hit the merchantman. In midafternoon a strike of bombers went after other anchorages, and one found a destroyer trying to escape. He dropped four 500-pound bombs on her, and was delighted to see the first hit in the wake, the next three walk the deck from stern to stem, and then see the ship covered in a mass of flame and smoke, dead in the water.

Mitscher was still full of tricks, and he saved one for late in the day. A strike went out with 1,000-pound bombs, but set with delayed action fuses, and planted them deep in the single runway of the bomber field at Moen. Another strike came in later, almost at the end of the day, and bombed the revetments of the fields. How right they had been to plan against an enemy night attack, because as they left they saw bomber after bomber going up in flame, which meant that those planes had full bomb loads and gas loads and were waiting to hit back at the task force. They would have some difficulty this night because the five big bombs were timed to go off at intervals during the night.

Although the fighters had been cleared from the air during the day, from somewhere that evening came more Zeros that hit the Americans hard. Some American planes were shot down. One *Enterprise* pilot, Woodie Hampton, had a very close call. The Japanese had observed that the Americans were using the island's Northeast Pass as a checkpoint and rendezvous for their attacks. Late in the day several Japanese planes congregated there to wait for American stragglers. Hampton was a straggler, and his plane was hit. He was limping toward the carrier, through the Pass, when he was jumped by three Japanese fighters. He shoved his throttle forward and ran, but the Hellcat was hurt and not flying at full speed, so the Japanese were all over him, making passes.

One of the Japanese got careless and came in too close, above and to port. Hampton swung up and to the left, and gave a brief burst of his fifty-caliber guns. The Japanese plane hung up there for a while, began to smoke, and rolled over and went down in a huge puff of black.

There were two more Japanese on Hampton's tail and he was saved from death by the armor plate behind his seat, but this was not very comfortable living. What to do? There was not a friendly plane in sight. He had an idea: he turned off his IFF switch, which meant that his plane would not be recognized by the Americans as friendly, and the combat air patrol from the carriers would be sent out to look him over. They would find the Japanese as well.

The idea was fine, but it was a long time in coming. Meanwhile, the Japanese were flying rings around him, just waiting. One came up on his tail and overshot, passing above. Hampton turned up and to the right and fired again. Down went the Zero. The third plane made a stern attack, and Hampton, with only three of his six guns firing, cut back his throttle, and as the enemy plane overshot, he jammed the throttle forward and took after him, shooting. The Japanese decided the plane was not so crippled after all and took off—and Hampton limped back to see the welcome sight of those wakes ahead of him. He could not make his carrier—the plane gave out before he got there, and he had to ditch alongside a destroyer. He was knocked out in the landing, and was very, very lucky, because the fighter floated long enough for swimmers to get to him and save him. Sometimes, sadly, the planes went down like rocks, and pilots who had made it back to the safety of the force went down with their planes.

So that was the first part of the strike against Truk, and Admiral Mitscher could be very pleased. He had found little there, but what was there was now in rotten condition compared with the way it had been in the morning.

So far successful day—but it was not yet over.

Mitscher maneuvered the carrier force east of Truk. The three carrier groups were within ten miles of each other—very close by old shiphandling standards. And as dark fell, the Japanese began to move around. For the next three hours, from 2100 to midnight, small groups of bogies appeared on the radar screens, keeping the men who ran the ships alert. *Yorktown* launched a night fighter to drive away the snoopers, but there was one group that would not be driven. It was a handful of Japanese bombers that were equipped with radar themselves, and they moved in against the carrier *Intrepid*, bombed, and scored one hit with a torpedo that sent a blinding flash of light above the fleet. *Intrepid* fought off the others and retired to Eniwetok at a speed of twenty knots, accompanied by the carrier *Cabot* and several other ships. She would have to go into drydock for major repairs.

But the difference of the fast carriers from the carrier fleets of the past was so great that the departure of two carriers did not seriously hamper Mitscher's operation or cause him to make many changes in his plan. That night he launched the first night carrier bombing attack in history.

The idea had originated on *Enterprise* with two young lieutenants who had been practicing bombing by radar contact. Lt. Henry Loomis and Lt. William Martin had discovered that they could go in almost to the beach in darkness and find their way by radar, then do the job and get home again. So in the wee hours of the morning the torpedo pilots of *Enterprise* assembled in the ready room for briefing. They had specially equipped torpedo bombers, and this was the big chance to use them. The briefing lasted an hour, and then came the familiar call: "Pilots, man your planes."

Just before four o'clock in the morning the flight crew moved to their planes, a dozen torpedo bombers, and boarded. Their target would be Truk at 500 feet, a destination eighty-six miles away. Flight leader this night, Lt. V. Van Eason, circled, burning his navigation lights to act as a beacon in the night as the bombers were catapulted (they were too heavy to take off by themselves loaded.) Three men in each of the torpedo bombers watched anxiously as the team formed up and headed toward the target. The moon was a half, riding two thirds of the way up the sky, the wind was warm and soft; in every way it was a delightful night in the tropics.

But not for the Japanese.

The bombers carried bombs, not torpedoes, each plane bearing four 500-pound general purpose bombs, with four-second fuses to allow the bombers a chance to get away from the low 500-foot level before they were blown up by their own weapons.

They picked up the reef on radar twenty miles out and moved north, around the edge of the reef, into the lagoon. They came to Northeast Pass, and here the formation broke up, with five planes stopping here to search and eight others cutting across the lagoon to the other main Truk anchorage.

The attack began at 0540, with radar operators in the planes directing the pilots to the targets. Suddenly a hospital ship lighted up, sending a glare across the water. A flare rose from somewhere; a searchlight began to stab the darkness.

The searchlight could be a problem. The pilots of these planes had to actually see their target to attack successfully, and if they were blinded by a searchlight they would lose their night vision for several minutes.

But Providence came to their rescue—Providence and the forethought of Admiral Mitscher. As the searchlight stabbed, a huge explosion rent the air; the searchlight went out. For a moment no one could figure out what had happened, but then several of the pilots realized that the explosion must have been one of the 1,000-pound bombs with delayed-action fuses dropped in the runway of the airfield the day before. The searchlight, close to the airfield, had responded as though someone was attacking the installation. So that danger was ended.

Then the bombers were attacking like foxes in a henhouse. They climbed to 1,000 feet, found targets, and headed down and in. At 250 feet they came, one minute apart, scouring the anchorages. Their operators watching the blips until the pilots could see the dark shapes come up ahead and beneath them. Then the operator saw the lineup and shouted "Mark." The pilot pressed the bomb release, and two bombs came tumbling out, one after the other. The delayed fuses gave time to swing up and around and get ready for the second run before the bombs went off. And one after another they came and came again.

A tanker erupted in flame, and lighted up other ships around it.

Antiaircraft guns began to chatter below and sent up golf balls of flame to find the planes.

The planes roared in, searching and finding. They dropped

their loads, then closed up the bomb bays and headed for the rendezvous point to reassemble and fly back to the ship.

Behind them they left two tankers and six freighters sunk, five freighters damaged. The smoke was still wafting upward as the morning fighter sweep passed the bombers over the lagoon. The bombers' job done, the fighters were coming in to begin theirs.

One plane did not come home, one only. The mission was an unqualified success.

The morning fighter sweep found very little but devastation when it moved in. Not a single Japanese fighter came up to oppose the F6Fs, and they spent their ammunition on the already devastated airfield and the sunken or burning ships.

There were three more strikes, hitting other ships. They sank a big tanker, and planes from *Enterprise* made a coordinated attack on the destroyer *Fumizuki*, which was racing along at twenty-seven knots, and sank her in ninety seconds. Other planes sank the destroyer *Oite*.

Aboard the flagship, Mitscher chuckled in that dry way of his because he had been as concerned about this raid as any of his pilots: since the first days of the war the very name of Truk had been synonymous with the fiercest of Japan's armed might.

"All I knew about Truk was what I'd read in the *National Geographic,*" Mitscher admitted *after* the raid.

They did not know exactly—carrier men seldom knew exactly—what they had accomplished. After the war the true success was learned: the carriers had the most successful operation of the war to date. They had sunk two light cruisers, four destroyers, three auxiliary cruisers, two submarine tenders, two subchasers, an armed trawler, a plane ferry, and twenty-four merchant ships, five of them tankers. They had destroyed 250 planes. They had lost 25 planes of their own, but most of the crewmen had been saved by submarines and seaplanes.

So the fast carrier task force was being welded into a juggernaut of a fighting unit, by the man who knew precisely how to do it—Marc Mitscher.

The admiral sat in his swivel chair on the bridge, watching

and waiting, and saying very little as his men rolled out these new ways of fighting that he was teaching them. Scarcely was the Truk raid over when he was heading elsewhere, first to a point southeast of the Marianas to refuel, and then in to hit the Marianas and find out what was there. After the Marshalls the Marianas was going to be the next big objective of the Central Pacific campaign.

Moving toward the Marianas, Admiral Mitscher was scouting new seas and penetrating further into Japanese territory than anyone had gone since the Tokyo raid. Always before the carrier men had insisted on the element of surprise in their attacks. Adm. Wilson Brown had made it a part of his carrier doctrine never to attack if the surprise element was destroyed; Admiral Fletcher had followed the same principle. But times had changed, and so had American air capability. Mitscher had some different ideas.

How different they were became apparent on the afternoon of February 21, when the task force, with six carriers, was heading in toward the Marianas. Suddenly a Japanese patrol bomber appeared out of nowhere. Before the combat air patrol could be vectored over to catch the bomber, it disappeared in the clouds and was not seen again. Worried intelligence officers rushed the word to Admiral Mitscher, who was curled up in his swivel chair, at peace with his world. They hurried because they knew what ought to happen—the admiral would be spooked and would hightail out of the area, because everyone knew a carrier could not stand up to land-based air-power in force, and the Japanese certainly would have a large force of airplanes in the Marianas.

Mitscher listened to the bad news. He was riding facing aft, as he often did, and he gave the officers who brought him the news no indication of what he was really thinking. He just sat there and looked out at the water.

Then came another message. Intelligence had just checked out a Japanese dispatch: the plane had definitely spotted them and sent the word, which would now be flashing along the Japanese air pipeline all the way to Tokyo, alerting planes and men.

Mitscher grinned his imp grin then, and gave his staff th word: "We will fight our way in."

Now the true power of the flattop brigade would be exh bited. If they could successfully negotiate this operation the could move anywhere in the Pacific. But could they? It ha never been tried, and there were men aboard the ships of th task force who thought it could not be done without sufferin serious losses.

Mitscher sat in his chair and talked a little. He predicted Japanese attack just after sunset. They would meet it wit antiaircraft fire—no night operations this time. He woul have liked to send up night fighters, but he did not hav enough trained men or the proper kinds of planes, heavy wit radar.

As darkness fell, twenty-nine ships swished through th Pacific, moving ahead, men watching and waiting, checkin their guns and ammunition, and looking anxiously into th horizon. But they did not see much—it was pitch dark befor the enemy came in, riding the phosphorescence of their wake as was the Japanese custom. And for the rest of the night ther was very little sleep for anyone, as the bogeys kept appearin on the screens. And yet when morning came, and the shootin stopped, not one carrier or any other ship had been hit. The had weathered the first attack.

In the morning Mitscher was ready to do some attacking. was February 22. "Today is Washington's birthday," he tol the task force. "Let's chop down a few Nip cherry trees."

Then they set out to hit the Marianas and test them fo strength. They pasted Guam, Saipan, Tinian, and Rota Is lands, smashing seventy planes and knocking another fifty one out of the air with a loss of six American planes. The they went home, with a bag full of photographs of the Mar ianas which Admiral Nimitz and Admiral Spruance would us in their final planning for the next invasion.

Mitscher was embroiled then in an altercation about whic he did not much care, the struggle between the airmen and th non-airmen for control of naval policy. One result of tha struggle had been an order from Admiral King that every tas force commander would hereafter have an opposite number a chief of staff: that is, if the commander was a surface ship man, he would have an airman as chief of staff: if he was an airman, his chief of staff would be a ship man.

The admiral did not like the order much, but in the navy men did not get to be admirals without learning to take an order in good grace, and he took this one. His outgoing chief of staff, Capt. Truman Joseph Hedding, brought him a list of names; characteristically, Mitscher said he did not give a damn who was chief of staff under these conditions, and so Hedding actually ended up selecting Capt. Arleigh Burke, a very competent and very daring destroyer commander who had won all kinds of honors by chasing and sinking Japanese destroyers in the South Pacific.

The relationship started out under something of a cloud; Burke did not much want to join a carrier task force, and Mitscher did not much want a "black shoe" as his chief of staff. In fact, when Burke reported, Mitscher was downright suspicious of the man. To an outsider it might have seemed that Mitscher was hoping that if he ignored Burke long enough, the destroyer man would dry up and blow away.

Burke was under a tremendous disadvantage—he had a boss who did not want him, and he was cast from the familiar world of ordinary ships into the complexity of a weapon of war that was still very new and very experimental. Mitscher ignored him completely, never offering a word of help about duty or tactics.

While this was going on Admiral Spruance decided to lead the Fifth Fleet, or Task Force 58, as it was called, into an attack on the Caroline Islands. Another first, another deep penetration into enemy territory.

On March 30 the attacks were to begin, and on March 29 they steamed into the reach of Japanese land-based air-power and came under attack. Burke began to take responsibility for maneuvering the task force, since no one else seemed to be doing it, and Mitscher seemed grudgingly to approve of what he was doing.

Palau was a tough nut. Admiral Nimitz wanted the harbor mined, and that was what was done. It was costly—the Japanese air fought back hard and twenty-five planes went into the drink, but twenty-six men of the forty-four who went down in them were saved by seaplanes, destroyers, and submarines. But Mitscher was not satisfied with this record; he would never be satisfied as long as his pilots and crew men were going down into the sea. For Mitscher was a sailor's admiral, he worried about his men and he did everything he could for them. Admiral Spruance, for example, was a cool, calculating strategist and master tacticion, but his relations with his officers and men were cool. He simply did not care about people as much; to him they were instruments to get the job done. Mitscher was like Halsey—he *cared,* and everyone aboard knew it, and they would fight for him or go anywhere for him.

Mitscher poked fun at Burke as a "black shoe." One day when a destroyer pulled up alongside the carrier on an errand Mitscher said to the Marine guard, "Secure Captain Burke until that destroyer gets away." And he wasn't smiling when he said it.

And once, during the landings of MacArthur's forces at Hollandia, when the task force was providing air support, he sent Burke out on a reconnaissance mission. Burke returned in a plane shot full of holes. "Thirty-one-knot Burke also reports he thinks the airplane is here to stay," said Mitscher.

Burke did not know what to make of these remarks, and neither did the rest of the Mitscher staff. Consequently Burke was a man in limbo, out of his element, walking on eggs all the time. It was a very difficult time.

Tension was released in a way by the rapidity with which they went from one operation to another. Hollandia was scarcely secured when Mitscher decided to try for another strike at Truk and received permission to do so. In they went, unmindful of the Japanese who scouted them long before they arrived: the fast carrier force was quite prepared now to operate under the noses of the Japanese.

Early on the morning of April 29 the Japanese found them and sent some forty-five planes in to bomb the task force. The enemy penetrated the fighter patrol and came after the carriers, but the antiaircraft men got them one by one. Then a Japanese submarine came along, and a destroyer knocked it off. Two bombers came in on *Lexington* and one got to within a hundred feet of the ship before it was hit; the other bombed, missed, and was chased off by fighters.

Mitscher shared another attribute with Halsey, one that made him a fearsome figure in the fleet. He hated the enemy with a real passion. Once a Japanese pilot prisoner was brought before him and said that he was disgraced and could never go back to Japan. "Too bad," said the admiral coldly. On another occasion after a fight, a destroyer rescued several Japanese out of water and announced it to the flagship. "Why?" asked Mitscher. These were the people who were killing his boys.

But in his eagerness to "kill Japs" a la Halsey, Mitscher did not leave stones unturned through haste or hate. He was precise and careful in his approach to the problems of war, as in the next big operation, which was to be the capture of the Marianas islands by the Marines with the support of the Fifth Fleet and particularly of Task Force 58, the fast carrier force. The job of the carriers was to prevent the enemy air force from doing anything to stop the invasion, and this meant destroying the enemy air-power, and knocking as much as possible the defense of Saipan, Iwo Jima and Chichi Jima.

Mitscher set out in June. Originally he planned to strike on June 12, but then he realized that all previous strikes of the fast carriers had been made at dawn. To cross up the enemy he struck first late on the afternoon of June 11 at these islands that stretched out like a snake 1,300 miles from Japan.

There were fifteen carriers for this fight, and as they headed into battle Mitscher was relaxed. He even joked with Burke now, and he sat on his bridge, eating ice cream and watching. He was sure of what he was doing.

The strike went out from the carriers, planes hitting Guam, Saipan, Tinian and Rota. They caught the Japanese unprepared, and destroyed 150 planes on the ground. Everything was going completely according to plan.

CHAPTER EIGHT

The Marianas Turkey Shoot

The Japanese had been most unfortunate in losing top naval officers to American air-power. Admiral Yamamoto's plane had actually been ambushed by American planes in the South Pacific, and after his death the new commander-in-chief was Admiral Koga, who lost his life in a plane over the Philippines. Then the new chief of the Imperial navy became Adm. Soemu Toyoda, whose task was the impossible one of winning a losing war.

As the United States prepared to attack the Marianas, the Japanese were aware of the shrinking perimeter of their Empire. They were aware also of the tremendous industrial might of the United States that was able to produce this army of aircraft carriers pitted against them, and the naval strategists saw nothing but trouble ahead.

Early in 1944 the Japanese concentrated all their hopes on their carrier force, and made Vice Adm. Jisaburo Ozawa, an air admiral, head of the fleet. Now the Japanese staked all their hopes on a decisive naval battle that they expected to win, thus stopping the Americans in mid-Pacific.

Ozawa was an experienced man. He was fifty-seven years old, slender, hawkfaced, and since 1942 he had commanded the Japanese carrier force. He had nine fine carriers, and the biggest and most powerful battleships in the world. Even this late in the war the Japanese fleet was something to contend with, and the Americans knew it. When the American invasion force hit Saipan on June 15, the Japanese were as ready as they could be to give battle, and Admiral Toyoda ordered

Ozawa and the fleet to go out and destroy the American force. That order set up one of the biggest naval air battles in the Pacific war.

The Japanese had been looking for this fight for a long time, and they had made careful preparations. Early in the year they had begun concentrating a carrier-oriented fleet at Tawi Tawi, southwest of Mindanao. By June 10 they had the nine carriers there, plus the two superbattleships *Yamato* and *Musashi*, three ordinary battleships, eleven heavy cruisers, two light cruisers, and twenty-eight destroyers. With a much smaller force than that, Admiral Spruance had put an end to the Japanese invasion of Midway two years before.

The Japanese fleet was actually at sea on training exercises when the American invasion of the Marianas began. Admiral Ozawa was aboard his flagship, the carrier *Taiho,* and on receipt of the message from Japanese naval headquarters, flags began running up the halyards of the carrier, and excited men began trouping back and forth to the flag bridge.

But what a different fleet than the one that had appeared at Pearl Harbor or at Midway! This fleet mounted about 430 planes altogether. Its pilots were eager and filled with the spirit of *Bushido*—they were ready to die for the Emperor. But those pilots were like the dive-bomber pilots at Midway Island itself two years before, when the Americans had not had enough training to do their job properly. This time the Japanese had been sent to sea, for someone must man the planes, although they had only a few hours in the air. But Ozawa pressed grimly on.

From the beginning the Americans knew the Japanese were up to something. The submarine *Redfin* had spotted the force moving into the Sulu Sea on June 13. On the 15th, coast watchers reported the force moving toward San Bernardino Strait, which splits the southern Philippines, and spotted other ships coming through Surigao Strait and moving east. It would seem that the Japanese were heading toward the Marianas to do battle.

Admiral Mitscher was delighted. There was nothing he wanted more than a face-to-face carrier encounter with the Japanese, to wipe out that enemy fleet once and for all. Admiral Spruance was not so pleased. He had just launched the largest American amphibious invasion yet tried in the Pacific war, and the Japanese move was endangering it. It was his feeling that the power of Task Force 58 must be used to protect and sustain the invasion at all costs.

The Japanese had several apparent advantages. The prevailing winds were at their bows as they came east, which meant that they could launch planes without any maneuvers at all, while the Americans would have to turn away from the enemy to launch, thus increasing the distance the fliers must make. The Japanese had airfields on all the important islands in the area, which meant they had places to land and refuel. They would be able to shuttle planes from carriers to attack and then to islands, a very handy system.

The Japanese air bases, after all, were no further away from Saipan than Guam, another of the Marianas, and at dusk on this June 15 Japanese planes took off from Guam and headed for the task force to strike the first blow of the battle. The planes were Zeros, the sleek fast fighters, and torpedo planes that went by the name of Frances. "Imagine them sending a Frances out to get *me*," grinned Mitscher, whose wife was named Frances. The Zeros were outclassed by the F6Fs, in pilots and in planes, and they were shot down very quickly as they approached. But the torpedo planes came in low, to stay below the horizon of the radar scopes until the last minute. This wavetop approach, plus the lowering darkness, let them get through the combat air patrol and come for the ships. As if they knew, they headed for *Lexington*, which was now Mitscher's flagship. The admiral sat on his bridge, riding backward. Captain Burke stood at his battle station on the starboard wing of the bridge, and the other members of the staff were at their various stations, wearing steel helmets. But not Mitscher. He almost always wore a long-billed flight cap, and he wore it today.

The torpedo planes bored in, five of them. Two dropped their "fish" even as they were being slammed into oblivion by the barking guns of the carrier. Those torpedoes came alongside on the starboard, so close that a man had to lean over the rail to see them. Then the other three planes came in, even though they were now hard hit and flaming. One came in over the bow, heading for the flight deck. But the burning pilot miscalculated, and the plane sped just above the deck and over into the sea—so close that several men swore the heat from the burning Frances singed their hair. Then the other two planes hissed into the sea, the three torpedoes passed harmlessly by, and the *Lexington* was safe for the moment.

At this point in the war, the young carrier admirals were agitating almost constantly to have their heads, to get the carriers freed from the responsibilities placed on them by higher authority so they could go out and chase the Japanese fleet. In a way it was like the attitude of the "hot pilots" of World War I who would do anything to go out and fight. They agitated again now, in the person of Rear Adm. J. W. Reeves, Jr., who suggested that the submarine hazard was great in the area, and that the carriers ought to move out and find Ozawa and smash him.

Mitscher replied: "YOUR SUGGESTIONS ARE GOOD BUT IRRITATING X I HAVE NO INTENTION OF PASSING THEM HIGHER UP X THEY CERTAINLY KNOW THE SITUATION BETTER THAN WE DO...."

That message was sent partly to quiet Reeves down, partly so that Admiral Spruance would see it and perhaps reconsider his decision that the carrier force should be used defensively.

On June 16 Admiral Ozawa slowed to fuel. Meanwhile, Admiral Mitscher put on a Mae West life preserver and was flown from the carrier to Aslito Field on Saipan for a meeting with Admiral Spruance and Adm. Richmond Kelly Turner, who was in charge of the landings on these islands. There Mitscher argued for an attack on the Japanese fleet, to knock it out before the Japanese could strike the Americans.

There certainly could not be any doubt about Japanese intentions, but Admiral Spruance was cautious. He simply did not have any information he trusted enough to act; he was asking for air searches from General MacArthur's land-based air-power in the Admiralty islands, but he got no word. All he had were the reports of the submarines, and sometimes the submarines had been wrong about their navigational fixes.

It was the afternoon of June 17 when Spruance issued his battle plan. It called for Mitscher and his carriers to knock out the Japanese carriers and the enemy battleships and cruisers. Then the fleet of new battleships, under Admiral "Ching" Lee, would engage the enemy and complete the destruction of the fleet.

So the task force moved, hunting the enemy, who was hunting the Americans.

Before dawn on June 18 Captain Burke woke up Admiral Mitscher and handed him a message. In a minute Mitscher was out of bed and joined the members of his staff at flag plot, where they figured the Japanese would be 660 miles from Saipan by dawn. By late afternoon, Mitscher could reach the enemy, and perhaps even make one attack. But the decision was up to Spruance, so Mitscher asked. Did Spruance want him to find the Japanese and attack, with a night engagement of the battleships to follow? If not, then Mitscher suggested they retire eastward by evening. The message also went to Lee.

Lee considered. He knew that the Japanese favored night engagement because of their training and skill. "Ching" Lee had just recently put together the fleet of fast battleships, and they had virtually no night training at all. To fight at night, even with American radar superiority, seemed to Lee to be a mistake. No, he did not want a night engagement.

Spruance had given Mitscher and Lee tactical control, and now Mitscher reluctantly decided that since Lee did not want to fight at night, they would have to turn away from the enemy. And, as Spruance announced that evening, he wanted the ships kept close to Saipan.

So they waited, and in the evening Mitscher turned away from the enemy.

Shortly before midnight Mitscher made another attempt to push the battle. He sent a message to Spruance saying he proposed to turn back west at 0130 in order to hit the enemy by 0500 on the morning of the 19th. Spruance acknowledged the message, and then Mitscher waited, sitting on the edge of the long couch, smoking.

He waited an hour until the message came in. "The change proposed in your message does not seem desirable." That was the answer. In the polite language between admirals, Spruance was saying no.

And in so saying, Spruance passed to the Japanese the chance to make the first strike, thus violating all carrier doctrine.

A member of Mitscher's staff said, "We knew we were going to have hell slugged out of us in the morning and we were making sure we were ready for it. We knew we couldn't reach them. We knew they could reach us . . ."

So Burke and the staff sat up all night, considering plans. Admiral Mitscher quietly went back to his bunk. He could not change the mind of the conservative Spruance; it was Spruance's responsibility, and that was all there was to it.

At dawn Mitscher was back in flag plot with the bleary look of a man who had not slept. Now he had to work out delicate timing, because every time the fleet wanted to launch planes, it had to move away from the enemy. And then, as if to add emphasis to how little Spruance knew about the carriers, came a message from the senior admiral suggesting that the carrier planes be used to neutralize the airfields on Guam and Rota. Spruance did not know—but Mitscher did—that the carriers had already expended a great proportion of their bombs and ammunition against air fields in preliminary strikes. Mitscher would save the rest for his fight against the Japanese fleet. He declined to send the planes.

At dawn the combat air patrols were out over the fleet, looking for the enemy. Mitscher had breakfast about 0630 and walked out moodily onto the bridge to see what he could. He said very little. His staff knew he was upset and disappointed at what he considered to be excessive timidity, but he never said a word about it. He was, as always, the controlled naval commander who knew his job and his place in the scheme of battle.

At dawn, the planes in the Japanese fleet were ready. The

sun rose red over a blue sea. There was scarcely a cloud in the sky, and the clever wind continued to blow for the Japanese at fourteen knots, coming from the east, so they could launch planes without changing course a jot. The morning reconnaissance found the Americans, and Admiral Ozawa had no hesitation: he ordered the attack. At 0730, seventy-three planes took off and headed for the American fleet. Meanwhile, on Guam, ten minutes or so earlier, a swarm of Japanese planes also took off. American fighters alerted the carriers, and F6Fs were launched from six carriers to head for Guam and engage the enemy. They moved in, sought battle, and in an hour had shot down thirty-five Japanese planes with a loss of one Hellcat.

They broke off the fight just before 1000, responding to an urgent call from Mitscher; the Japanese from the enemy carrier force were coming in. At 1004 the warning bells clanged aboard the *Lexington* and the bugler blew his general quarters call over the public address system. The battle was about to begin.

Men raced along the passages and clumped up and down the stairs; watertight doors slammed with a clashing sound, and then squeaked as the dogs were set. Men ran across the flight deck, shirts fluttering in the wind. Engines coughed and spat and flames shot out from their exhausts. Pilots sat in the ready rooms, absorbing last-minute information. On the bridge sat Admiral Mitscher, watching the flight deck.

The bombers were sent off out of the way, so the fighters could have full use of the decks of the carriers. Out at sea, some of those fighters sent away from Guam were already engaging the Japanese attackers. They shot down plane after plane—but not all of them.

Lt. Comdr. C. W. Brewer of *Essex* was in the thick of this first battle of the fleets. He led a flight against the incoming Japanese, found the leader of the Japanese formation and began shooting at him from 800 feet. The Japanese plane exploded. Brewer pulled up on the tail of another; it fell flaming into the sea. He chased a third and his bullets went into the wing roots until the plane flamed and crashed. He was chased by a Zero, but rolled and got on its tail and went into a dogfight marked by barrel rolls, wingovers and loops. The superior speed and maneuverability of the F6F paid off; he caught the Japanese plane and started it burning, until it winged over and crashed in a spin.

Twenty-five of those Japanese planes were shot down in this encounter, but some got through. One bomber scored a hit on *South Dakota,* killing twenty-seven men and wounding twenty-three more. One just missed *Minneapolis.* But that was all. The raid was broken up and the planes either headed toward Guam to land and refuel or went back to their carriers. There were very few to return at all.

The Japanese launched a second wave at 0800—and 129 more planes headed out for the American fleet. At 0830 a third wave took off.

The American carriers were seeing action in every way. After that first big fight, Admiral Mitscher recalled the bombers that were orbiting out east and had them drop their bombs on the runways of Guam and Rota on the way back. That made life more difficult for the Japanese pilots who got away. Then around 1100 a new crop of Japanese planes showed up to attack the fleet. Off went the fighters again, vectored out by the fighter director.

"Hell," said one pilot, "this is like an old-time turkey shoot"—and the battle had its name.

For the Americans, superior in every way today, this was a turkey shoot. For three hours, until 1430, one raid after another was met by the F6Fs, and the planes were shot down, one by one. Admiral Mitscher stayed on his bridge, taking reports from pilots and staff members on the progress of the battle. Torpedoes came in, but *Lexington* dodged them. Japanese planes zipped by, most of them under attack and already on their way into the drink.

So the Americans fought a defensive battle, as demanded by Admiral Spruance. Only around 1500, when it was apparent to everyone that several hundred Japanese planes had been shot down and that Admiral Ozawa had lost his offensive capability, did the fleet commander release the carriers to strike at the enemy.

But by that time the Japanese were already in serious trouble. Before 1100 the carrier *Taiho* had been hit by a submarine torpedo. What a lucky shot it was, for the torpedo broached the aviation gasoline lines in the ship, loosing the vapor, and the *Taiho* exploded not long after Admiral Ozawa got off in a destroyer to move his flag to the cruiser *Haguro*. And then, about twenty minutes later, *Shokaku*, that survivor of Pearl Harbor, was hit by two torpedoes; she caught fire, burned, and sank.

By late afternoon Admiral Ozawa had only about 100 planes left, and he decided to withdraw to the northwest to reorganize. The Americans, bottled up all day, could not find the Japanese, and as evening fell Mitscher had little hope of finding them at all. He conferred with Captain Burke, never mentioning his extreme disappointment at the conduct of the battle, and then early in the evening he went into his sea cabin and went to bed.

Next morning the fliers of the fleet were eager to go out and find the enemy, and there was no dearth of volunteers for the job. It would be risky—it would mean about a 50-50 chance of getting back—but Comdr. Ernest Snowden insisted on leading the flight, and the volunteers were eager. The search was launched at noon, and went out 475 miles, the longest search of the war. They found nothing. But as they were heading home a plane from *Enterprise* did find the Japanese, and the attack was on.

It was very late in the day—the first planes were not launched to strike until 1630—and at the distance of the Japanese fleet, more than 300 miles away, the planes would strain to the last of their gasoline on the way home, and would have to land in darkness. Mitscher let the one strike go, but canceled all the others until the next day.

Admiral Ozawa had shifted his flag again, to the carrier *Zuikaku*, and he fought as valiantly as he could. The few planes went up, and were shot down. The bombers arrived about 1820. They torpedoed *Hiyo*, the light carrier, and her steering was jammed. That made her an easier target for another torpedo, and she blew up at 1932. Another light carrier, *Junyo*, took two bombs and six near misses that raised hob-with her plates, but she survived. Light carriers *Ryujo* and *Chiyoda* were damaged by near misses, and a battleship and a cruiser were hurt; also, two supply ships were sunk.

Some Japanese were shot down, but most of them ran out of gas and landed in the ocean. The Japanese fleet had no time to come and get them, so they perished in the sea, pilots and crews of some eighty planes.

So the First Battle of the Philippine Sea, as it was called officially, was over that night. Admiral Ozawa headed back for the safety of Okinawa, his victory plan smashed to pieces. But one could not say that about his fleet, for the Americans had chosen not to give battle fleet to fleet. Admiral Spruance's reason was that he had a primary obligation to support and protect the landings in the Marianas. But the carrier men never ceased to believe that he had let the Japanese fleet get away, and that if he had let Admiral Mitscher have his head, Mitscher would have smashed Ozawa so that the Japanese could never put a carrier fleet to sea again.

The battle was over, and as such it was won. But as night began to fall over the American task force, Admiral Mitscher stood on his bridge, and he was more concerned than at any other time during the whole fight. His boys were out there— eighty-five fighters, seventy-seven dive-bombers, and fifty-four torpedo planes. He had sent them out, knowing that if they had enough fuel to get home, they would have just barely enough. And now he doubted if they were going to make it.

Mitscher stayed on the bridge, eating his dinner on a tray. He kept looking at his watch. He changed the fleet around, spreading the task groups fifteen miles apart so the pilots would have a better chance of finding a carrier.

As darkness fell the pilots were still about seventy miles out, and their gas tanks were running dry. Admiral Mitscher faced a disaster—what if none of those planes—more than 200 of them—got home? He speeded up the fleet and headed toward the planes.

At 2030 the first planes came into sight, beginning to orbit over the task force. But they could not stay up long; their gas must be almost exhausted.

There was one cardinal rule of naval fighting in this war, and a very simple one: he who showed a light at sea endangered himself and the fleet. Who knew how many Japanese submarines might lie around them? The Japanese submarines had been more active lately, and more successful. It was a very definite threat.

But there was only one way to save the pilots of those planes out in the air, running out of gas. Mitscher did not hesitate.

"Turn on the lights," he said.

And Task Force 58 leaped out from the darkness, some searchlight beams flashing through the sky, others pointed at the carrier decks, outlining them for all to see. Cruisers threw up a succession of star shells, silhouetting the whole fleet. And on the ships the men began to cheer when they saw what their admiral was doing to save his boys. They cheered and shouted and clapped each other on the back as the planes began to come in.

"Tell 'em to land on any carrier," said Mitscher. And they did. Some settled in—six came in on *Lexington*, and then one plane crashed into the barrier, and the wreckage had to be cleared away quickly. Any delay at all was serious. Planes were running out of gas, pilots were landing alongside destroyers and battleships and carriers, close by so they would be seen and picked up. As the planes came in they crowded the deck, and the captains ordered the crowding planes pushed over the side to save those airmen.

It was all over by 2230. Of the 216 planes that had taken off, 100 landed. Of the others, perhaps twenty were casualties of the battle, and nearly 100 went into the sea or were destroyed in accidents on landing.

Mitscher headed the fleet toward the place where the Japanese had been, and ran fast. Next morning more pilots were picked up, and in the end, all but sixteen pilots and twenty-two crew were saved from this dangerous mission.

From that day on, in the carrier fleet, Marc Mitscher could do no wrong.

CHAPTER NINE

Halsey Again

In addition to the attempt to force the naval issue at the Marianas, the Japanese had taken several other actions by the summer of 1944. They had moved some ships to Lingga Roads, off Singapore, and this move had frightened the British into keeping their navy to protect India, rather than sending ships to the Southwest Pacific to join MacArthur's forces, as had once been planned. The Japanese had also begun an offensive in China that would cut off the Chinese armies and the American air force stationed in China from the southeast area where they came near the coast. The defeat of the Chinese seriously weakened the navy plan for a landing in Formosa to be followed by one in China. Still, by July 1, 1944, the matter was undecided. The navy had a plan, called Granite II, which still called for landings on Formosa and China. General MacArthur had a variation of his basically undeviating plan, called Reno V (this was its fifth revision) that called for invasion of Mindanao, then Leyte, then Luzon, with a target date for capture of Manila in the spring of 1945.

One of the preliminary operations was to be the seizure of the Palau Islands.

Halsey had been relieved of what was becoming a routine job as commander of the South Pacific by June 1944 and had been brought to Pearl Harbor to begin planning the Palau invasion. There was a new element in this planning: Halsey and his staff decided there would be no fixed schedule of strikes or operations for the fast carrier forces.

Here is how he put it:

"The initial strikes covering the Palaus operation would be launched against the Mindanao section and from there on tacitly among the staff and between the staff and the commander was the agreement that we would look the situation over and examine the enemy's reaction to determine what next, and we kept an open mind. If resistance was greater than intelligence indicated, we might have to stay there and slug it out, but if we found weakness we considered that there was to be no limit to the geographical distance we would go to carry out our job of exerting military pressure on the Japanese empire."

This concept was new, and it was to change the practice of naval warfare and throw confusion into the Japanese at a crucial moment.

By July Halsey was planning to seize the southern Palaus on September 15, and about three weeks later to seize Yap and Ulithi Atoll. Halsey never stopped thinking of one idea: "that mobility of the striking and covering forces should be maintained, exploiting enemy weaknesses and seizing every opportunity that offered or could be created to destroy major units of the Japanese fleet." The ships began coming in, from the Marianas, from the repair yards, and from the shipyards. The principal unit of the Third Fleet was to be Task Force 38, which would be specifically under command of Vice Adm. Marc A. Mitscher. Task Force 38 consisted of four Task Groups, the carrier fighting unit: Task Group 38.1 under Vice Adm. John S. McCain in *Wasp;* Task Group 38.2 under Rear Adm. G. F. Bogan in *Bunker Hill;* Task Group 38.3 under Rear Adm. Frederick C. Sherman in *Essex;* and Task Group 38.4 under Rear Adm. Ralph E. Davison in *Franklin.* Together the striking force consisted of nine fleet carriers, eight light carriers, six battleships, thirteen cruisers, and fifty-eight destroyers. Each carrier had its own air group, consisting of fighter planes, dive-bombers, and torpedo bombers. The big carriers would have about forty fighters, thirty-five dive-bombers and eighteen torpedo bombers; the small carriers, about twenty-three fighters and ten torpedo bombers. In other words, the striking force consisted of *more than 1,000 planes.*

Halsey assembled his fleet, planned, and prepared. Then,

on August 28, he sailed out from Eniwetok to soften up the objectives.

Davison's task group was sent to hit Chichi Jima and Iwo Jima in the Bonin Islands for three days beginning August 31. Then Davison moved to Yap, and his planes bombed and strafed Japanese installations there on September 7 and 8. Halsey took the rest of the task force to the Palaus and hit there hard from September 6 to 8. Then he moved away, leaving the next strike to Davison, and also letting Davison cover the support of the invasion on September 15 and 16.

Halsey moved over to the Philippines and hit Mindanao beginning on September 9. A convoy of sampans and small cargo vessels was sighted, and several of the cruisers and destroyers were detached to wreck them. This was the high spot of the day, because Halsey's fliers were finding very little in the way of grounded airplanes to hit on the airfields. Following his theory of ranging far and wide, Halsey moved over to the Visayas on September 12, and again found very little opposition, so little that he decided the Western Carolines were not even needed, except Ulithi, which provided an excellent fleet anchorage. This opinion was confirmed when one of McCain's boys, Ensign Thomas C. Tillar, was shot down off Leyte and then rescued by Filipinos who told him there was no Japanese strength in the Leyte area. Tillar's report got to Halsey and capped everything else the admiral had learned. On September 13, Halsey sent a radio dispatch to Admiral Nimitz, suggesting that all the current landings be canceled as unnecessary, and that the next move be against Leyte. It was less than two days before the scheduled landings on Morotai and Peleliu.

Admiral Nimitz did not agree to cancel these landings, but in his careful way he passed on the suggestion in messages to Admiral King in Washington and to General MacArthur in the Southwest Pacific. The idea was accepted.

At sea, Halsey was busy. On September 14 Admiral McCain's carrier group was sent to hit Mindanao and sweep the Celebes area. It encountered no airborne opposition, which increased Halsey's confidence. The Davison and Bogan groups flew direct air support missions on the Palau invasion.

Halsey came up to the area to order that Wilkinson seize Ulithi Atoll, and to pay a visit in his flagship *New Jersey* to the Peleliu operation. Everything was going very well. Halsey was planning ahead. The Ulithi base would become the center of Pacific fleet operations in the months to come.

Everywhere the Third Fleet went, its men found signs of Japanese deterioration in the Philippines. On September 21 the Third Fleet's carriers tried a new technique, explained by Admiral Carney, Halsey's chief of staff: "There was an almost universal opinion that carrier aircraft could not be employed against strongly entrenched land-based air. That opinion was not subscribed to by Commander, Third Fleet."

No, Halsey believed that by hitting hard in pinpoint attacks against specific objectives he could outweigh the power and maneuverability of land-based air. Also, in Carney's words, "We therefore felt that in the case of enemy Army aviation that we could deal with them very nicely, and we knew that their most formidable Navy aviation groups had been broken up long ago and were being manned by an inferior type of pilot; he was still dangerous, but not as dangerous as he had been."

So Halsey moved his carriers in to the east coast of Luzon, north of Polillo, under the cover of squalls and rain—and achieved complete surprise against the Luzon airfields, catching many planes on the ground. "They were caught with their kimonos up," said Carney. Within two or three hours of the first strike, air opposition on Luzon virtually disappeared in the attacks on the fields. Then the Third Fleet's planes turned to merchant ships, docks, oil storage tanks, and anything that seemed interesting around the waterfront. They played a mean trick on the submarine U.S.S. *Lapon*, too. That submarine was off Luzon, stalking a Japanese convoy of merchant ships, escorted by small war vessels. Her captain was waiting to shoot when suddenly out of the sky swooped the planes of the Third Fleet, which sunk his merchant ships and left him nothing but the escorts. Nimitz got into the action then, from long distance. Following very carefully what Halsey was doing, Admiral Nimitz suggested that in view of Halsey's successful strike on the Manila area, Japanese shipping would be diverted, and specifically indicated that they ought to try Coron Bay. They did, on September 24, using mostly fighters carrying bombs, and sank twenty-three ships and damaged another fifty-four vessels.

Halsey then ordered the ships of the Third Fleet into Manus, Saipan, and Ulithi, which had been occupied without opposition on September 23. He had some planning to do, too, because the fast carrier forces of his fleet were being used in a way never tried before, and some new ideas were in order. One was unique: a refueling technique in which each carrier task group was assigned an opposite group of tankers, and at the appointed time for refueling the support ships moved into a formation alongside the fighting formation that put each ship in position with its opposite number. The escort carrier replacement ships, which carried planes for the fleet carriers, would come in at the same time and launch planes that would land on the flight decks of the fleet carriers.

Some days were devoted to solving problems of this nature, and then the Third Fleet went out again to pursue its part of the overall plan. Its mission early in October was to knock out as much enemy air support as possible. This did not simply mean hitting the Philippines and surrounding islands, because the Americans had now breached the perimeter of the inner Japanese defenses, and the air resupply method of the Japanese was to fly planes from Japan, island-hopping to Luzon.

The Third Fleet was hampered a bit by a typhoon that formed near Ulithi on October 3, but on October 6 the fleet was at sea once again, and the ships rendezvoused on October 7 west of the Marianas. The next day the refueling plan was put into effect in high seas left over from the typhoon that had just passed by.

The following day Halsey's first diversion went into effect. Rear Adm. A. E. Smith took three cruisers and half a dozen destroyers and bombarded Marcus Island, approaching under the cover of bad weather. They spent the whole day lurking about the island to persuade the Japanese that the next American invasion would be in the Bonins. But the Japanese were much more interested in what was to come. On October 10 the carriers hit Okinawa and destroyed 100 planes, then wrecked as much of the airfield facilities as they could. They also sank every ship in sight in the nearly 1,400 flights made that day. This was by far the closest to the Japanese homeland that American fliers had come since the spring day in 1942 when Halsey had sent the B-25s of Lt. Col. Jimmy Doolittle on their way from one of his carriers. The raid alerted the Japanese defenders of the interior of the Empire.

The Japanese report of these raids showed what was happening to Japan's air strength: "At 0640 [October 10] 400 planes began raiding Okinawa and nearby islands, striking four times between then and 1600."

That was the beginning of the great air battle of the islands, the battle that would have the utmost possible effect on the plans of the Japanese—turning them just enough awry to change their entire focus.

Three days before the beginning of this battle, Admiral Toyoda, the commander-in-chief, went to the Philippines with several members of his staff. He was dead certain that the Philippines would be invaded next and very soon, and his visit was primarily for morale purposes, to encourage the defenders. First he went to Manila and met with the commanders there, Vice Admiral Mikawa, commander of the Southwest Area Fleet, Vice Admiral Teraoka, commander of the First Air Fleet, General Terauchi, commander of the Southern Army, and General Yamashita, who had been brought in recently to command the Fourteenth Army that would do so much of the fighting on the islands.

Toyoda had planned to visit the southern islands to see the troops and installations on Cebu, Davao, and Tacloban. But when he reached Manila he found that American air attacks were coming so frequently·and there were so many planes in the air that he could not travel in his transport without an escort of half a dozen fighters. There weren't enough fighters anyhow, and he could hardly justify taking them away. Then he caught cold, went to bed for three days, and ended up seeing nothing but Manila.

On October 9, Toyoda's transport flew back to Formosa,

en route to Tokyo. He wanted to get back the next day to Hiyoshi, his Combined Fleet Headquarters, where his staff was stationed and his communications were located.

Then came the morning of October 10.

When Toyoda heard the first reports of the huge attack on Okinawa and the outer islands, he knew what was coming. Halsey was unleashing the power of the Third Fleet to do just what Toyoda and the Japanese planners expected him to do; sweep all the region to knock out Japanese air.

At that moment what Toyoda wanted more than anything else was to be at his post in Hiyoshi, near Tokyo. Here he was on Formosa with only three members of his staff, in a spot where communications were unequal to his responsibilities. All the intelligence reports were going in to Hiyoshi, and he could not see them. He did not know what was going on, literally, except what he saw in the skies above him.

When the attacks on Okinawa began that morning, Combined Fleet asked the admiral what should be done. Should he activate the SHO operations (the last-ditch stand of Japan's navy,) for the air forces only? That would mean the commitment of all operational planes to the big air battle.

Toyoda could not answer the question from where he was. He gave the responsibility to his chief of staff back at Hiyoshi. The chief of staff decided to activate. At 0930 came the word of warning, and at noon the 51st Air Squadron and the Third Air Fleet were ordered down from the northeast of Japan to the Kyushu area.

It was 1540 on October 10 before the Japanese patrol planes found the "enemy force." What they discovered was less than a third of the force: five carriers and ten vessels identified as cruisers. They planned an attack with a pitiful little force of five attack planes and four flying boats to go in at night, but decided against it.

At 2100 on the night of October 10, Japanese flying boats equipped with radar were out prowling in the vicinity of Okinawa and Formosa, but it was 0300 on the morning of the 11th before they found an American force, and then it was 2 o'clock that afternoon when American planes, fifty or sixty of them, raided Engano and Aparri on the northern end of Luzon. The Japanese were confused, for they kept sighting task forces with multiple carriers, and yet that day there was no other attack.

On October 11, Halsey had decided on a feint against Luzon, which he had hoped would persuade the Japanese to look to the Philippines for a time. It was a small fighter sweep, involving only about sixty planes. It did some minor damage, knocking out a dozen planes on the ground, but that was all.

The plan called for the carriers and their escort to retire from the Luzon area and turn toward Formosa, reaching a striking position at dawn on October 12. They would hit Formosa for two days, then retire. By the evening of the 13th, Halsey expected to have knocked out the Japanese air potential for resupplying the Philippines from Formosa.

The four carrier groups ranged themselves around the island that morning of October 12, and in the good, windy weather began launching planes, less than 100 miles from the Formosan coast.

The Japanese confusion continued as the four task groups kept well spread out. At 0240 on October 12 the Japanese flying boats were out again, three of them, and one plane located a task group "which included several aircraft carriers" about 180 miles off the Formosa coast. This report and others began to come together, and the Japanese came to the conclusion that the Americans were operating in five separate groups. At 0340 on October 12 the air raids began sounding at Japanese installations throughout Formosa.

The confusion ended at 0648, when an estimated 600 planes swarmed across Formosa, north and south from these carriers. Takao port took it hard—several merchant ships were sunk very quickly, and the Dakao naval construction yard was badly smashed. In the confusion of the 11th the SHO operation had been more or less suspended—nothing was done to implement it—but at 1030 on October 12 Combined Fleet Headquarters, putting its intelligence altogether, had ordered the carrier planes that were either on the carriers or en route to them to be diverted to the Second Air Fleet to fight the battles of Luzon and Formosa. Admiral Toyoda, a prisoner on Formosa, could only sit and watch and listen, so thoroughly was he cut off from the implements of command. The Japanese were not sure where or when the invasion was coming, and the plans activated were both SHO 1 (Philippines) and SHO 2 (Formosa). Now the Second Air Fleet, including these Third and Fourth Carrier Squadrons robbed from the carriers, moved to southern Kyushu and began the move to Formosa. Kanoya was the staging point, and from here in the evening patrol planes located three American task groups, northeast, east, and southeast of Formosa. They were hampered by very bad flying weather that evening; a typhoon was passing by to the east.

The harassment of the Formosan airfields continued all day long, and nearly 200 Japanese planes were destroyed, in the air and on the ground. The Japanese retaliated in some force in the evening, sending over a special attack force of torpedo bombers. And now began a strange development, later described by Admiral Carney:

"The fighter patrols over our forces shot down tremendous numbers of Japanese planes and those that came in were, for the most part, destroyed by the automatic weapons of the ships.

"When this happened at dusk . . . a very peculiar situation developed. Japanese planes were being sprayed around the ocean as they burst into flames on crashing, tremendous fires flared up on the surface. These were interpreted by other Japanese pilots to be American ships destroyed by the suicide attacks. These interpretations and the reports of the Japanese pilots made were undoubtedly made in good faith. It is a well-known fact that pilot observation of types and of damage is not to be trusted either by our own forces or by the enemy's."

Typhoon or not, fifty-six planes, bearing the cream of the Japanese aviation groups—the T Force—took off from Kanoya and attacked the American task forces from 1900 to 2020. Some, not many, of those planes came back, and thus began the legend that was to guide the Japanese onto entirely the wrong track in the days to come. The surviving planes, most of them shot up, came back in disorder and landed where they could, all over Formosa. Intelligence officers learned from the pilots that they had sunk ships. Putting together stray bits of information from many sources, the optimistic intelligence officers decided the pilots had sunk four American carriers that night. Elated, the commanders sent out a night bombing force of twenty-three carrier planes and twenty-two bombers, which attacked at midnight. Those who came back said they could not determine the enemy losses.

Next day, October 13, the First Air Fleet in the Philippines got into action. The Americans were still striking Formosa in strength, catching some Japanese planes on the ground, but not many. The big destruction had come the day before in the surprise attack.

Thirty planes of the special T Force attacked one carrier force, saw four carriers, and claimed to have sunk two ships, including one destroyer. The same planes at 1834 hit another force with two carriers. The visibility was spotty and usually poor; the American ships were moving in and out of squalls, but the T Force pilots came back to claim having set fire to another carrier, and having seen still another listing badly.

Meanwhile, a force of 170 planes was put together on Luzon and started out for the scene of action, but was forced by bad weather to return to Clark Field.

The Americans made another 1,000 operational flights. That evening the carrier *Franklin* of Admiral Davison's group very nearly took a Japanese bomber aboard. The plane came in, out of control after having been hit, caught fire, and slid completely across the carrier's flight deck, trailing flames, and then went over the side. To any Japanese pilot watching, it must have seemed that the *Franklin* had suffered a mortal blow. Actually, the damage was so light that Halsey did not even include the incident in his fleet operational report to Admiral Nimitz.

But that same evening a more serious event occurred: the cruiser *Canberra* was torpedoed and badly damaged. There was question for a time as to whether or not she could be saved, but the damage control parties isolated her flooded fire-rooms, and although she was dead in the water, Halsey decided to take the chance of towing the cruiser home. To cover the exercise, he ordered another strike that was not in the plans for the next day, on Luzon and on Formosa, while the cruiser *Wichita* took *Canberra* under tow and headed for safety.

On October 14 the Japanese attacked in great force. "The Nips decided to throw everything they had in the way of air attack against our forces," said Carney. "The attacks took the form of formations of from sixty to eighty planes, but those of us who had seen the air operations earlier in the war in the South Pacific were immediately impressed by the fact that these aerial formations were nondescript in character, included all types of planes, and that the technical performance was not nearly of the same order as had been previously encountered."

Most of these planes were destroyed, burning and splashing, until at the end of the day the Japanese had lost some 500 aircraft in this three-day air battle. But at 1845 the cruiser *Houston* took a torpedo, and another American ship was soon dead in the water. At first she was to be abandoned, but the captain changed his mind, and before long the cruiser *Boston* took her in tow, too.

The Japanese jumped to all the wrong conclusions. They took the decreased number of planes raiding that day to mean confirmation of the "tremendous damage" they were doing to the Americans. The planes struck between 0700 and 0930, and then it seemed that the task force was withdrawing to the southeast.

Sensing weakness the Japanese threw everything they had at the carriers: "Our entire air strength of approximately 450 planes which had completed deployment in Southern Kyushu, attacked this task force three times [during the day, at dusk, and at night]. Here were the results the pilots claimed: at 1525 a force of 124 planes claimed one carrier; at 2000 a force of 70 planes claimed one battleship."

Now came another complication for the Japanese. A hundred B-29s, which the Japanese thought came from China, hit Tainan and Takao. Many of the planes that had been attacking the American fleet had come into these fields, and they were caught on the ground. Damage was extremely heavy, in loss of planes, fuel, ammunition, and parts and repair facilities at all the fields.

In spite of these high losses, no one called off the Japanese attack. Admiral Toyoda was out of touch, and the staff at Hiyoshi was either mesmerized by the reports of sinking so many American ships, or afraid to question the reports of the brave T Force airmen. So the sacrifice went on.

Halsey's damaged cruisers *Canberra* and *Houston* and their escorts were identified on October 15 about 260 miles off Takao and a force went out to hit them, but bad weather sent the Japanese back to base. But Combined Fleet Headquarters was not finished yet. From Hiyoshi came exhortations to the Japanese airmen to rush in and "finish the job" because so much damage had been done the Americans. All day long the Japanese threw their planes at the American forces, and the few straggling pilots to return came back with heroic stories, as that of Rear Adm. Masabumi Arima, commander of the Clark air base and the 26th air flotilla, who went out himself to sink a big ship. He did not return, and the Japanese who were with him who did come back told a brave story of Admiral Arima diving his land-based attack plane into an American carrier.

October 15 ended, and Combined Fleet added up its results in the magnificent air battle staged by its air forces:

Strike No.

12 October	1	Four ships sunk, believed to be carriers
	2	Ten ships set on fire
	2	Two ships set on fire
13 October	1	Two carriers and two other ships sunk
		One carrier set on fire

14 October	1	One carrier and three cruisers set afire
	2	No results
	3	Two carriers, one battleship, and one heavy cruiser sunk. One carrier, one battleship, and one light cruiser set afire
15 October	1	One carrier sunk
	2	Two carriers set on fire. One cruiser damaged

The reports, such as those that follow, were to have a tremendous psychological effect on the commanders of both sides in the next few days to come.

"Extra! Extra! Extra!"—said the Radio Tokyo broadcast to Greater East Asia at 10 P.M. on October 15. "The Imperial Fleet has finally made its appearance.

"As mentioned in the Imperial Headquarters communiqué at 3 P.M. today the Imperial Forces carried out repeated fierce attacks on the main strength of the enemy task force detected in waters east of Formosa and have already achieved the result of nine aircraft carriers sunk or damaged, one destroyer sunk, one battleship sunk, one cruiser sunk, and eleven unidentified ships severely damaged.... It is evident that the main strength of the enemy task force has been almost completely annihilated. Besides the Imperial Air Forces, the Imperial Naval Fleet is also included in the attacking force."

Another report said: "The enemy task force, which has been dealt a thoroughgoing defeat, is at this moment heading straight eastward.... The American navy, which to date has rescued its plane and ship crew members, due to the great defeat at this time is barely managing to make its escape in a confused manner." Still another gave American losses as "fifty-three carriers and warships so far sunk or seriously damaged ... even the most conservative estimates based on the losses of American war vessels ... puts enemy personnel losses at 13,000 and the loss of aircraft at 600."

At home the Japanese were delighted, and from the Emperor down they believed what they wanted to believe, that the American advance had now been halted, the mighty American carrier fleet crippled.

The Japanese continued to pursue the "fleeing" Americans from the air. This fact, and the knowledge that the Japanese could be persuaded to use their fleet, as Radio Tokyo indicated, gave Halsey an idea. He would use his two crippled cruisers as bait, and clean up at least a section of the enemy fleet when they came to kill the cripples.

Admiral Davison's task group was sent to make strikes on the airfields of Luzon, to keep Japanese air power down in that direction and give the impression that the Americans were moving away and would not strike Formosa again. Admiral McCain's group covered the two stricken cruisers and their towing companions. Admiral Bogan and Admiral Sherman withdrew to the east, to set a trap for any Japanese naval vessels that might come out. Later McCain was sent to join them, to make the cripples look even more inviting to the enemy. All the while American ships were transmitting what Halsey called "urgent messages" to create the appearance of desperation.

It was quite a group, under Rear Adm. L. T. DuBose. It was now called the Bait Division, and it consisted of seven cruisers, two light carriers and a number of destroyers. Obviously it was this force that the Japanese saw milling around and looking beaten, as Halsey wanted.

The ruse very nearly succeeded. The elated Japanese continued the air strikes on October 16. They also sent out a combined cruiser-destroyer force, Admiral Shima's Second Striking Force, to wipe out the enemy. Shima was steaming toward the Americans on the morning of October 15, when he was attacked by two planes from Bogan's carrier *Bunker Hill*. The planes were driven away safely, but Shima was concerned and later retired. In the afternoon Japanese searchplanes discovered the Bogan and Sherman groups, and the Shima force was called back, told to put into the Ryukyus, fuel, and then go south to the Pescadores, west of Formosa, to await further orders. The Japanese continued to press the air attack from

Formosa, and that afternoon a Japanese plane managed to put another torpedo into *Houston,* but still she did not sink. The battle ended on October 16. Halsey had accomplished more than he knew.

For all this, the official records showed, the Japanese lost only ninety-four planes. But then, on October 16, the picture at Combined Fleet Headquarters changed: "On the 16th, however, our reconnaissance planes sighted four enemy aircraft carriers 600 miles northeast of Manila, two carriers 260 miles and 110 degrees off Takao, and seven carriers 430 miles off 95 degrees off Takao."

There was no arguing with these clear reports. "Consequently," said the official report, "the results . . . were considered doubtful."

On October 16, Japanese planes were still out, buzzing as angrily as bees whose nest has been destroyed, but they did not locate the Americans, who were preparing to support the Leyte landings. On the 17th the Japanese were out again, and their patrol planes found four different groups of carriers, and this day they also discovered the force that included *Canberra* and *Houston* under tow. Headquarters ordered an attack, but it was never carried out.

All this time, Admiral Toyoda had been grounded on Formosa, gaining what information he could.

What Toyoda never discovered, or if he did discover it, he was unable to face and understand it, was that with these tremendously effective raids Halsey and his carriers had knocked out Japanese air-power in Formosa and the Philippines. Thus in the big battle of Leyte Gulf to come, the Japanese fleet would for all practical purposes be destroyed.

The Battle of Leyte Gulf itself was a triumph of American arms and combined air- and sea-power. The Japanese surface fleet charged in, broken into four sections, to stop the American invasion of Leyte, but the carriers again smashed that fleet.

The air battle began on October 24, early in the morning, after planes of the carrier *Intrepid* saw the main Japanese section off the southern cost of Mindoro Island in the Sibuyan

Sea, heading for San Bernardino Strait. The plan was for this force under Admiral Kurita to smash the American invasion.

As soon as Halsey heard that the Japanese fleet was coming, he acted. For months he had been waiting for a chance to strike that fleet. In his admiral's quarters on the *New Jersey*, Halsey had a game board built, and he and his staff had spent many hours dreaming up battles against the Japanese fleet. Here now was much of that fleet, including the superbattleship *Yamato*, and he wanted it.

So the four task groups, with all their might, were called into action. Just after nine o'clock in the morning a strike of twenty-one fighters, twelve dive-bombers and twelve torpedo planes left the carriers *Cabot* and *Intrepid*. More followed, until 259 sorties were made against the Kurita force that day. They sank the superbattleship *Musashi*, which had eighteen-inch guns. They damaged the other big battleships *Yamato* and *Nagato*.

Still that force went on into battle, four battleships, six heavy cruisers, two light cruisers, and eleven destroyers. It was not the only force. Two lesser groups of ships were coming up from the south, through Surigao Strait. They were attacked by planes that day, but the surface vessels smashed them on the night of October 24-25, until the tiny remainder turned around and headed back for Japanese territory.

Another force was at sea, consisting of what was left of the Japanese air might, a pitiful remnant that included the carrier *Zuikaku*, that veteran of the war since Pearl Harbor, the light carriers *Zuiho*, *Chitose*, and *Chiyoda*, and two very strange ships, the *Ise* and the *Hyuga*. These last had been battleships, but in the need for carriers it was decided to make a kind of carrier of them, so they were sawed off abaft amidships, and a flight deck was put on each of them. They were not particularly apt conversions, but there they were.

For all these carriers, the Japanese had only 52 Zero fighters, 28 converted Zeros (now bombers), 25 torpedo bombers, and 11 other bombers, or 166 planes in all.

The purpose of this force, led south from Japan by Admiral Ozawa of the Imperial Navy, was to divert Halsey and his

Third Fleet from the Kurita force that was coming through the middle, so Kurita could smash the American invasion of Leyte. In order to do so, Ozawa had to call Halsey's attention to his presence with the carrier planes, and managed this on the morning of October 24, sending a seventy-six-plane strike against Admiral Sherman's task group. Not one of those planes returned to the carriers; the ones that were not shot down landed at Japanese bases in the Philippines.

But what did happen—and what Ozawa wanted—was that Halsey found him, and accepted the bait. It was natural for Halsey to do so: he did not know that the Japanese air might had been destroyed in the Formosa air battle, and that planes destined for these Japanese carriers had been shot down much earlier. He did know that carriers posed the greatest threat to the American fleet of any ships, and he did know that to destroy Japan's carrier might was to end her naval prospects altogether. So Halsey decided on the night of October 24 that instead of staying by the American landings in Leyte Gulf, he would go out north to find Ozawa and destroy him.

Admiral Halsey said, "Searches by my carrier planes revealed the presence of the northern carrier force on the afternoon of 24 October, which completed the picture of all enemy naval forces. As it seemed childish to me to guard statically San Bernardino Strait, I concentrated Task Force 38 during the night and steamed north to attack the northern force at dawn. I believed that the Center Force [Kurita] had been so heavily damaged in the Sibuyan Sea that it could no longer be considered a serious menace to Seventh Fleet."

So off Halsey went.

The next thing anyone knew, Admiral Kurita came through San Bernardino Strait and started after the invasion fleet. All that stood between him and the troops and the transports were the small, slow, highly vulnerable escort carriers and a handful of destroyers.

The little "jeep" carriers did their very best. The pilots flew off and bombed and strafed the Japanese, and then landed and took off again. When the carriers were under attack and unable to care for their planes, the pilots flew to Leyte, landed there and took off again. For hours some of them circled above the Japanese, making false passes, unable to shoot because they had exhausted even their guns, but diverting the enemy like bees buzzing around the head of a bear.

The fight lasted just over an hour and a half, with the carriers trying to run away from the fast battleships and cruisers of the Japanese force, but also trying to divert them from the beaches at Leyte and the transport ships. Several of the carriers were hit. *Fanshaw Bay* took four eight-inch shells. *White Plains* was hit repeatedly. *Kitkun Bay* was damaged by near misses. *Kalinin Bay* bore the full force of Japanese attack from a battleship. But *Gambier Bay* was the unlucky one, and she was sunk by the Japanese.

The day was saved by the destroyers and destroyer escorts, which rushed in with torpedo attacks against the Japanese so fiercely the enemy mistook them for cruisers. At the end of it the Japanese were driven back with heavy losses of cruisers and destroyers, and limped home to the Dutch East Indies, from where they had come.

CHAPTER TEN

Cape Engano

On the evening of October 25, Admiral Mitscher was a very unhappy man. Admiral Halsey had just sent a message indicating that he was taking over tactical control of the task force. That was his right as commander of the fleet, but it did not make Mitscher or his staff feel any better to know that Halsey was now making the decisions.

"Admiral Halsey is in command now," said Mitscher, and got up from his seat in flag plot to go to his cabin for the night.

Captain Burke stopped him. "We'd better see where the fleet is," he said. He meant the Kurita force, which was even then steaming toward San Bernardino Strait.

"Yes," said Admiral Mitscher. Each knew what the other was thinking, that the Kurita force might well be very dangerous. They knew that Halsey had already made the decision to head north toward the force of carriers and other ships commanded by Admiral Ozawa. They also thought Halsey ought to leave some ships at San Bernardino Strait to guard against Kurita.

Just before midnight a plane reported that Kurita was indeed headed for San Bernardino Strait. Burke woke Mitscher.

"We'd better tell Halsey to turn around," he said, for the task force was already heading to do battle in the north.

"Does Admiral Halsey have that report?" asked Mitscher.

"Yes, he does."

"If he wants my advice he'll ask for it," said Admiral Mitscher, and he rolled over in bed.

131

So the fleet steamed on to engage the Japanese, while the Kurita force moved in to do its job at San Bernardino Strait.

At 0205 a search plane launched from the *Independence* found Ozawa's fleet about eighty miles north of the task force. The battleships moved out ten miles ahead of the carriers to protect the big flattops from attack by surface vessels.

At dawn the strikes began. The planes took off from the American carriers. Now they learned that the Japanese had turned during the night and were now 140 miles away, speeding north. Ozawa's purpose was to draw the Americans away from Leyte, and he was succeeding.

Mitscher's pilots hurried out to find the enemy, and then they reported. Four carriers and two battleship-carriers, and many other ships. They began their bombing, practically unhampered by fighter opposition, because Ozawa had sent off almost all his meager supply of planes in the strike the day before.

If the First Battle of the Philippine Sea had been a Turkey Shoot, then this was a stag hunt, with the hounds unleashed on the stags at close bay.

Ozawa had only about a dozen planes up to protect his fleet, and he had to rely on his antiaircraft guns. *Zuiho*, the light carrier, had a few planes on her decks, and as the Americans bored in she tried to pull out and launch. Planes came in from *Essex* and *Lexington*. The torpedo bombers missed her, but an *Intrepid* dive-bomber got her and she broke away, still very much a fighting machine. But the light carrier *Chitose* took several bomb hits and began to sink. *Zuikaku* took a torpedo that knocked out her communications, so Admiral Ozawa moved to the cruiser *Oyodo*. A Japanese destroyer was sunk. Most of the Japanese planes were knocked down in this first stage of the battle.

The second strike from the American task force made bomb hits on the light carrier *Chiyoda*, and she began to burn and list. At 1018 a bomb knocked out her engines. The battleship-carrier *Hyuga* tried to take her in tow. Just then in came strike number three, so *Chiyoda* was abandoned, dead in the water.

The third strike went after the fourteen ships still afloat, including *Zuikaku*, *Zuiho*, and the two battleship-carriers, *Hyuga* and *Ise*. The *Lexington*'s planes concentrated on *Zuikaku*. *Essex*'s took *Zuiho*, and *Langley*'s planes split up between the two. Both carriers began to burn, and soon *Zuikaku* turned over and sank. Then *Zuiho* tried to get away, streaming smoke and fire, but about eighty planes went after her and she sank, too.

The next attack concentrated on *Ise*, but the aim was not very good and the Americans got only thirty-four near misses with bombs. *Ise*'s captain threw up an intense barrage of anti-aircraft fire, and she maneuvered very well. *Hyuga*, the other battleship-carrier, fared even better. She got only seven near misses all day, although the planes took after her, too.

In all, the Americans flew six strikes that day, 527 plane sorties, and they sank four carriers and a destroyer. Admiral Ozawa did not think much of the Americans' shooting. "I saw all this bombing," he said, "and thought the American pilot is not so good." Perhaps. But he had been good enough to destroy the Japanese carrier air force on this final day when *Zuikaku* went down, obliterating the memory of Pearl Harbor, and realizing one of Admiral Nimitz' fondest dreams—to knock out all the carriers that had done the job on December 7, 1941.

Ozawa had never really expected to go home again from this battle, for he knew from the outset that his force was to be the sacrifice that would let Kurita get in among the American transports at Leyte Gulf. But Ozawa did go home, with his battleship-carriers and a handful of cruisers and destroyers, to limp into the naval yard and put the ships up for repairs.

Halsey, meanwhile, had been called for help by Admiral Kincaid back at Leyte Gulf, and he had responded with the fast battleships and part of the carrier force. As it turned out, he was too late to help at Leyte Gulf, and the battle was all over by the time he got back. By turning around when he did, he let Ozawa get away when the fast battleships could have annihilated what was left of the Japanese fleet.

* * *

But it did not make much difference, because the destruction of that fleet was so nearly complete by October 25, 1944. The carrier war had now become completely one-sided.

The fleet went back to the anchorage at Ulithi for rest and recuperation from this hard time at sea. On the way, on October 29, the carrier *Intrepid* was hit by something quite new in this war, a *Kamikaze* suicide pilot. This new idea brought something damaging to the sea war, not just to carriers, but to all planes. The Japanese were particularly interested in sinking the carriers and went after them, but they also hit others.

As for Mitscher, at Ulithi, the new fleet anchorage to replace Pearl Harbor and Eniwetok as the take-off points for the war, he debarked from his flagship to go home for a rest. Adm. John S. McCain would replace him in command of the fast carriers for a while.

On October 31, 1944, the word was passed around the *Lexington* that the admiral was leaving in the morning. And he did, at 0400. In spite of the dark and the chill, most of his pilots got up and came to see the admiral off, for he represented something special to them.

After his leaving, after Leyte, the carrier war changed a great deal, for there no longer was any Japanese fleet to contend with, to bring caution to the hearts of the overall commanders of amphibious operations. Hereafter the carriers could range at will around the seas of the enemy Empire.

CHAPTER ELEVEN

The Death of the Japanese Fleet

When one looks at the losses of the Battle of Leyte the disparity is so great that it is remarkable the Japanese admirals could have any hope left at all for anything. Japan lost three battleships, a fleet and three light carriers, six cruisers, four light cruisers, and eleven destroyers in the four forces that took part in the battle.

Now it became for the Ameican carriers a question of tracking down and destroying the units of the Japanese fleet as they found them, and the emphasis naturally had to turn to tankers, supply ships, and other shipping because there was (with one great exception) to be no further Japanese naval effort on the sea. The Japanese navy fliers in the Philippines, for example, became troops or Kamikaze pilots.

October 1944 marked a high point in American aerial attacks on Japanese shipping and caused the Japanese to change their manner of protecting shipping between the outer fringes of the Empire and Japan proper.

By November, the results of the Leyte battles had brought about a basic change in the convoy system. Convoys had been routed from Southeast Asia along the Philippines to Japan, but now they hugged the Asiatic coast instead. The convoys became smaller, and the number of destroyers and escorts were increased. There was even an occasional cruiser along. Japan absolutely had to have oil above all, and there was only one source of supply to her, the Netherlands East Indies.

The story of just one convoy at the end of the year is indicative of what was happening to Japan's forces at sea in these last terrible days.

Capt. Chuji Kawamura was the commander of the tanker *Sarawak,* a 5,000-ton ship that plied between Singapore and Japanese ports bringing oil and aviation gasoline. Between November 20, 1943, and the summer of 1944 she made three trips to Singapore and back; then on the fourth trip sixty feet of the ship's bow was blown off and she was towed to Manila. In August 1944 the ship was taken to Japan, and in the middle of December repairs were completed there. Captain Kawamura sailed from Yokohama on December 31, bound again for Singapore to bring back gasoline. There was a decided difference this time.

There were ten merchant ships in the convoy and eight escorts. This was hardly an economic way to use shipping, but Japan was desperate for petroleum products.

The speed of the convoy was twelve knots, sailing out of Moji. When it was learned from convoy command that U.S. Task Force 58 was in the South China Sea, plans were changed, although the convoy was ready to hug the China coast. It was diverted to Takao.

On January 8 the first ship was sunk by a submarine off Keeling, Formosa. Then, in Takao, in harbor no less, the convoy was attacked by Task Force 38's carrier planes on January 9, and three more ships were sunk. One ship also suffered engine trouble and was lost to the convoy here.

The air attack began in the morning, and came over in four waves that day—the Japanese estimated 300 planes in all. They sank or damaged two other ships in the harbor besides those of the convoy, dropping perhaps 100 bombs and then strafing. A ship 200 yards from the *Sarawak* was sunk. Captain Kawamura's men manned their twelve machine guns—there were fifty navy men in his crew these days. The American bomb marksmanship was not very good, but perhaps that was because of the terrible weather in Takao that day; it was so cloudy that the Japanese in their ships could not see the Americans until just before they dropped their bombs

—and, of course, it worked both ways. They were flying in at 600 feet to drop.

On January 10, the convoy was now reduced to five tankers and cargo ships, plus the escorts. It sailed from Takao, followed the China coast in shallow water past Hong Kong, and was passing outside Hainan Island—or beginning to. When the convoy reached a point just north of Hainan, the leader had news that Task Force 58 was moving north again through the China Sea, and so the convoy turned and headed for Hong Kong. It reached the harbor on January 13. But on January 15 and 16 the carrier planes came in again and attacked the convoy in Hong Kong harbor, sinking four of the five cargo ships in the convoy. Three hundred planes a day came in. At the end of the raid, of the cargo ships and tankers only *Sarawak* was still afloat, and six escort vessels had been damaged.

At the end of this second day, Captain Kawamura's ship had only about 200 rounds of antiaircraft ammunition left. He consulted with the convoy commander, and they discussed what the next day might bring. If the task force planes came back, almost certainly the ship would be sunk. Perhaps, said the commander, it would be a good idea to fill the ship's tanks with water to make it appear that she was half sunk. That way the Americans might ignore her and concentrate on other vessels.

But the staff of Task Force 58 figured they had done enough damage to Hong Kong in two days' bombing, and moved on. On January 17 *Sarawak* and four escorts left the harbor and proceeded down the China coast, north of Hainan, following Hainan's coast to the port of Yulin, stopping there and then going on the next day. The ships cut directly across to the Indo-China coast that day, hugging the shore and shallow water to keep submarines off at least one side. Down they went to Saigon, then to Pointe de Camau, the southernmost point of Indo-China, and then back across to the Malaya coast—all this to avoid attack.

What happened? Just off the coast of Malaya the convoy was attacked by a submarine, and one escort ship was torpedoed. It was January 24. The escort fell out, and the three

other escorts and the *Sarawak* went on toward Singapore
Straits, where they anchored on the night of January 26. That
night B-29s dropped mines in Singapore Straits, near the anchorage, and the next morning when trying to get into port,
Sarawak hit a mine. Not only was she damaged, but she had
to sit and wait four days for the navy to come and sweep the
channel, so she got into harbor on January 31. It was mid-
February before she was in drydock, and March 15 before she
was repaired and ready to sail. One ship of ten had made it
back to Singapore to pick up supplies for the Island Kingdom
on this voyage!

On March 19, *Sarawak* was loaded with diesel oil. She
joined a convoy of five other ships and six escorts. There
were three tankers, and other ships loaded with supplies. They
began bravely, but just outside Singapore, in the main channel
near Horsburg light, *Sarawak* struck another mine, which put
a hole in the engine room. Towing began, but she sank on the
way and was a total loss. Thus, not one of that convoy of ten
ships sent from Japan ever returned. And as for the rest of that
convoy—not one of the ships ever arrived in Hong Kong.
All, tankers, cargo ships, and escorts, were sunk off the coast
of Indo-China. It was the last convoy from Singapore.

Militarily speaking, the Japanese continued to do a consid-
erable amount of damage to American ships all during the rest
of the war, by far the greatest part of it accomplished by the
suicide craft. For example, on October 29, the carrier *Intrepid*
was hit, and on the 30th *Franklin* and *Belleau Wood* both
suffered serious damage from Kamikazes. A month later, four
American carriers were badly damaged by suicide planes.

The Third Fleet continued to harry Japanese shipping (and
when it was not the Third Fleet it was the Fifth Fleet—same
ships and same planes, but different fleet commanders). It
was the Third Fleet that caused the almost total destruction of
Captain Kawamura's convoy in January in Formosan waters.
And they were doing the same everywhere they could. Here is
a paragraph from the carrier reports of January 12, 1945,
which gives some indication of what was happening in Asian
waters.

"No major ships of the enemy were found, but the air

strikes of 12 January on the French Indo-China coast achieved more shipping destruction. One enemy convoy was entirely destroyed and two others severely mauled; the shipping tally totalled 41 ships (127,000 tons) sunk and 28 (70,000 tons) damaged; among ships sunk were two cruisers, one Japanese (*Kashii*) and one French (*Lamotte Picquet*), partially dismantled, at Saigon; docks, oil storage, and airfield facilities were heavily damaged; 112 enemy planes were destroyed, the Indo-China coast was left a shambles. Air opposition was negligible; the CAP destroyed practically all of 50 enemy reinforcing planes ferried in on the afternoon of the 12th . . ."

On January 13 and 14 the Americans destroyed 38,000 tons of Japanese shipping.

On January 16 the planes destroyed 88,000 tons of shipping. They hit Formosa again, but they noticed that when they came within the inner Empire or fought off the Philippines where the Japanese were still putting up strong aerial resistance, the Americans took a series of blows from the Kamikazes. On January 21 the fleet hit Formosa and destroyed 200 Japanese planes. This was of course felt in the Philippines. It narrowed the pipeline through which planes were ferried. But the Kamikazes got to *Ticonderoga* and *Langley* and the destroyer *Maddox,* and *Ticonderoga* and *Maddox* had to be sent back to the base at Ulithi for repairs. On January 22, Third Fleet became Fifth Fleet with the advent of Admiral Spruance as commander, but the destruction of Japanese ships and navy went on. Fifth Fleet—Third Fleet; that is the way it alternated until the end of the war, and little by little, one by one, the carrier groups and land-based air-power sought out the remnants of the Japanese fleet, and destroyed those ships one by one.

Many of the Japanese ships fell to submarines. One big Japanese ship to go that way was *Shinano*, the world's supercarrier, a ship on which the optimistic among the Japanese still managed to place an almost miraculous hope for the future of ending the war.

Shinano was first planned as a superbattleship of the *Yamato* class. But after the Battle of Midway, when Japan lost four big carriers, Admiral Yamamoto and others of the air admirals persuaded the navy to change over the design and plan to produce the supercarrier.

That was in June 1942.

What with the change in plans and the exigencies of war and shortages of steel that began building up with the success of the American submarine effort, *Shinano* was not finished until November 1944. She was everything promised: with a special flight deck and a capacity of seventy planes, she displaced 71,000 tons and bristled with machine guns and antiaircraft guns. Her flight deck was a composition of steel and concrete that was supposed to resist any aerial attack, no matter how strong or prolonged.

On November 11, Armistice Day—ironic as it may seem —*Shinano* was launched in Tokyo Bay, and although usually several months were devoted to fitting out a carrier, or any other ship, she was quickly commissioned and thrown together with a green crew, many of whom had not been to sea before in any vessel. The admirals were grasping at straws. Perhaps this great carrier, impervious, they said, to air attack, could sail bravely out and engage the terrible American task force that now had its way around the Japanese islands when it appeared. Perhaps *Shinano* could sink Halsey and Spruance and Mitscher and all the rest of those hated Americans, sink them and send them to the bottom forever to rot among the sands.

Even before she had loaded all her equipment, *Shinano* was dispatched to Shikoku, which was the central training center of the Combined Fleet. She was trained, or they said she was, and was made ready to rush into battle. With *Yamato* and the lesser ships that could be assembled, and with *Ise* and *Hyuga* (which were under repair), Japan theoretically could mount a formidable fleet, particularly if the enormous threat of *Shinano* was added. No one knew what she might do in battle.

On the evening of November 28, *Shinano* set out, accompanied by three battle-weathered destroyers, on her maiden voyage. She was only traveling from Yokosuka to Osaka Bay. Three years ago, even one year ago, this had been sacrosanct water, and an American submarine that dared enter risked the life of every man without much hope of accomplishing anything in exchange. But times had changed; American submarines were everywhere, it seemed, and an American submarine found *Shinano* and her escorts. The submarine was the *Archerfish*, and her captain was Comdr. J. F. Enright, who was stationed on lifeguard patrol to aid and comfort the B-29s that were flying from the Marianas over Japan these days. He was basically stationed 100 miles south of Tokyo Bay, but on this day he had been given a holiday (no bombing raids scheduled) and he was roaming around looking for excitement.

Shinano, and destroyers *Hamokaze*, *Isokaze*, and *Yukikaze* were steaming out on this cold evening under a bright chilled moon when just before nine o'clock they were sighted by *Archerfish*. They were nervous enough already: an hour before there had been a submarine alert, and the ships were zigzagging and alert. This was no accident, no carelessness, but the confrontation of two deadly weapons, the carrier and the modern submarine of the day.

Commander Enright surfaced and chased the fast-moving group—they were making at least twenty knots and the only reason he could keep up and then gain was that they were zigzagging on a base course, which cut down their forward speed.

And then the submarine alert ended, and the group resumed its southern course—with a change that brought it right into the tubes of *Archerfish*. Capt. Toshio Abe could not have been more unlucky. Captain Enright could not have had better luck.

On they came to a point 1,400 yards away from *Archerfish*, which only had to lie there and shoot, then dive deep to escape the expected depth-charging.

Four torpedoes struck home, tearing a great hole in the *Shinano*'s center on the port side. No pumps could stop the water, no mattresses or shoring could rebuild that shell. And then, although she could and did steam south at twenty knots for a way, the watertight compartments gave way, or were not dogged properly, or leaked—because *Shinano* settled and listed, and it became apparent that she was going down.

Lieutenant Sawamoto heard the order to abandon ship, but

instead of rushing to the side he took the Emperor's portrait from the captain's quarters and gave it to a seaman in the water. Lieutenant Sawamoto was not seen again.

Captain Abe stayed on his bridge, and near him stayed Tadashi Yasuda, the top graduating man in his class of 1943 at the naval academy. Both went down on the bridge.

It was just as well for Captain Abe, because he had believed too well what the designers told him about the carrier's unsinkability. He might have made port and saved his ship, but he did not believe she could sink—until eight hours after the torpedoing, on the morning of November 29, when she went down, carrying him and 500 men who did not get off. *Shinano* never launched a single plane.

And then there was *Junyo*, that survivor of the Marianas turkey shoot. Just after midnight on December 8, 1944, the U.S.S. *Redfish*, a submarine, was chasing a convoy and was sighted by one of the escort vessels. *Sea Devil* was on the other side and apparently firing, because *Redfish* heard two explosions just before the time came to move away. The chase of the destroyer was not long, but by one o'clock in the morning *Redfish* was far enough away that only a zig by the convoy would help put her in position to fire torpedoes.

From the *Redfish* records:

"0130 Convoy is pulling away from us and only a miracle will bring it back.

"0134 The miracle arrives! Heard two separate explosions far enough apart to be two torpedo hits. Aircraft carrier slows down. Gives a big zig toward. He must be hurt! This attack, if made by a submarine, came as a complete surprise to us and we had been searching without success for radar interference ahead in the hopes there was someone up there to turn the convoy toward us.

"0137 Another explosion

"0139 Another explosion

"0140 Another explosion.

"0142 Aircraft carrier is now dropping well astern of the other ships and we are closing fast.

"0156 Carrier has speed up to 12 knots angle on bow 110

range 2900 commenced firing six air torpedoes forward at least one of which made an erratic circular run.

"0158.10 Heard and saw one terrific hit in carrier—also saw destroyer passing between carrier and us on opposite course. He was just coming back to screen carrier from battleship group when we started firing.

"0159.30 Another explosion. Flash seen from bridge, but unable to tell whether it was a torpedo hit in carrier."

Between 0201 in the morning and 0211 there were no fewer than seven explosions heard by *Redfish*, and her captain began working around for more shots at this convoy. He wanted to sink the damaged carrier.

By 3 o'clock *Redfish* was having difficulties. She was nearing the 100-fathom curve off Nagasaki; that would mean minefields inside, and visibility was growing much too good. Also, the carrier was not hurt as badly as she might have been and still had plenty of speed. The destroyers were very, very wary.

Twenty minutes later *Redfish* attacked, fired ten torpedoes, and heard three explosions. And then a little more than an hour later *Redfish* intercepted a message from *Plaice* that said she had been the other submarine attacking from the other side. Whether she hit the carrier or destroyers or both was not determined just then. But what was determined was that the wolf pack had got *Junyo*. Another Japanese capital ship was damaged so severely that she was out of the war.

"It has been quite a night," said the captain of *Redfish*. "Feel bad about not sinking that carrier, but maybe he'll blow up before he hits port."

He did not blow up, but he did not go out again, either.

And *Redfish* had her moment of glory a few days later off the China coast.

At about four o'clock in the afternoon, *Redfish* sighted masts.

Just before four thirty the captain saw two destroyers and a carrier. He did not know it, but it was the *Unryu*.

He moved in:

"1629 Target has zigged toward angle on bow 30 starboard —changed speed to 1/3—flooded bow and stern tubes. Can make out three escorting destroyers. One ahead and one on each bow of target.

"1635 Commenced firing four torpedoes from bow tubes (all we had forward). . . .

"1635.45 First torpedo hit causing target to stop, list 20 degrees to starboard, and commence burning aft. Target opened fire just prior to being hit, with all guns on starboard side. . . ."

The starboard escort came around astern. *Redfish* fired several torpedoes but did not know if she got a hit. Then she was too busy to notice much because the destroyers came after her. But they milled around and did not find her, so she got into position and fired an electric torpedo, hitting aft of the carrier's island.

"Torpedo hit carrier at point of aim. The sharp crack of the torpedo explosion was followed instantly by thundering explosions apparently from magazine or gasoline stowage, probably the latter. Huge clouds of smoke, flame and debris burst into the air completely enveloping the carrier. When Executive Officer looked several seconds later he still could not see the ship due to the smoke."

They began changing course to avoid the milling destroyers. At 1656 the executive officer, looking through the camera of No. 2 periscope, saw the target listing heavily, stern submerged, with many planes on deck.

So *Unryu*, another proud carrier, had gone to the bottom with her deckload of planes.

The planes of the fast carrier force did much damage to the shore installations and shipping in Japanese waters now. For example, on March 19, carrier *Ryuho* was hit so hard in a raid on Kure by planes of the task force that she was inoperational for the rest of the war.

Seeing such damage, and knowing what was happening, that the Japanese navy was being swallowed inch by inch, Admiral Toyoda and the high command planned Operation Kikusui, named for the fourteenth century Japanese patriot Masashige Kusunoki, who led his soldiers to certain death in the battle of Minatogawa so that Japan's spirit might survive. Kikusui was to be a series of operations, ten of them in all, largely involving the Kamikazes at Okinawa, where the

Americans were expected to land next. But there was a new coordination; the navy would send its fairest flowers out to fight this time on a suicide mission similar to that of the Kamikazes. It was planned that way.

The Americans did land on Okinawa on April 1. The naval force consisted of so many ships it would be almost too much to have expected the Japanese to believe them if they saw them. The gunfire and covering force of big ships alone consisted of ten battleships, eleven heavy cruisers, and a fleet of destroyers. The escort carriers numbered fourteen, with a swarm of destroyers, and there were no fewer than seventeen fleet carriers and light carriers, with all the new battleships and the cruisers and the scores of destroyers. This was just to defend the landing forces against whatever the Japanese might put up.

What the Japanese proposed to put up were the 700 airplanes they had available for attack on the American forces right then, and the strength of the fleet in inland waters.

On paper the Japanese fleet was still a formidable weapon. As of the first few months of 1945, the Americans thought it consisted of four battleships and the carriers *Unryu* (sunk), *Amagi*, *Katsuragi*, and *Ryuho*.

What the Japanese actually did have in home waters were the battleship *Haruna*, the battleship-carriers *Ise*, *Hyuga*, the battleship *Nagato*, and the superbattleship *Yamato*.

The carrier *Amagi* was afloat, and so were *Katsuragi* and *Hosho*.

Of the cruisers there were *Aoba* and *Ashigara*, *Tone*, *Kitagami*, *Yahagi*, and *Oyoda*, *Sakawa* and *Kashima*.

Admiral Toyoda and his staff had placed *Yamato*, *Yahagi*, and eight destroyers in a command unit, the Second Fleet. And on April 5, after the Americans had landed at Okinawa, the Japanese were sending a battleship and cruiser and eight destroyers on a suicide mission.

The Japanese naval reasoning is very specious here, but the idea generally was to attract the enemy air to the *Yamato*, as flies to honey, and thus take the attention off the island so the proud army defenders could counterattack during this time and wipe the Americans off Okinawa.

When the operational orders were read to the skippers of

the ten ships, only the captain of *Yamato* failed to object. The others all had the same idea: why destroy a fleet and its men simply for such an object?

"This operation does not offer us a proper place to die," objected Capt. Kiichi Shintani. "A more fitting place will present itself when we can engage the enemy in hand-to-hand combat as we oppose his invasion of the homeland. The proposed plan is idiocy!"

Another captain suggested that Combined Fleet staff come out of its air raid shelter at Hiyoshi and fight the battle itself —which was about as close to mutinous talk as one ever heard in the Imperial navy, particularly when voiced in front of the chief of staff of Combined Fleet, as the captain's suggestion had been.

When the word was out, the seamen aboard the ships began sharpening their bayonets, for they had been told that if they once got among the American ships and did their job, then they might get ashore and join the army fighting for the defense of the homeland. They did not know that they would first have to swim through some 1,200 American ships. That night the crew got sake and salty biscuits called sembes, and celebrated the coming heroic operation. That night they also jettisoned everything burnable and not needed on this last voyage of the fleet: wooden objects, paints, canvas, even the ship's boats. A group of midshipmen, straight out of the naval academy, were sent ashore objecting fiercely that they too should be allowed to give their lives for their country.

Aboard the *Yahagi*, Adm. Keizo Komura entertained his captains with sake, and they drank many bottles, and threw them into the sea, singing patriotic songs from their naval academy days, and thinking of the morrow.

And on that morrow, at 1500, there sailed from the Inland Sea the strongest force that Japan could put together at that moment, with *Nagato* under repair, two cruisers in the south, and *Haruna* repaired. For two days *Yamato* had moved to avoid snoopers but now, as they moved out, they were snooped by B-29s and by enemy submarines going through Bungo Suido.

The fleet moved on majestically, past Tanegushima and

Yakushima, and at six o'clock in the morning entered the open sea. At the same time, the Japanese Kamikazes were harrying the American fleet off Okinawa, and hitting a dozen ships with varying degrees of destruction. The Kikusui operation was in full-sway, and oddly enough the Japanese seemed to have learned nothing from the failure of Kurita at Leyte. But Tokyo, perhaps, hoped to distract Americans. Tokyo was also interested in maintaining the Japanese fighting spirit to the end, and it was through such sacrifices as this one, that seem so needless to the Western mind, that the Japanese would accomplish their aim.

Early on the morning of April 7 a few Japanese planes circled the fleet, but soon they were gone, along with the seaplanes of *Yamato* and *Yahagi.* Planes, as potential Kamikaze weapons, were too valuable to be wasted. In this topsy-turvy world of Japan's only the greatest battleship in the world could be wasted needlessly.

Meanwhile, American submarines had been shadowing the tiny fleet, and *Hackleback* reported her whereabouts. In the morning the Japanese were tracked as they came in circular formation zigzagging into battle. And Admiral Mitscher's search planes were out.

At 0823 that morning an *Essex* plane found the Japanese and sent a report on their course and speed. Admiral Mitscher told Admiral Spruance, who asked Adm. N. L. Deyo if he wanted to take the ships. So few were they, so little the risk to the Americans, that it was like playing a game. It was nothing like the battles of Leyte. There was something languid, and a bit supercilious even, about the American approach to the problem. One could not blame them; their superiority was such that the issue was not in doubt from the moment the Japanese ships sailed. The only question was who was going to dispose of these gnats.

Admiral Mitscher's boys were hungry. Task Force 58 began to put forth its strike planes, and here is the story of what happened next from the report of Air Group 10 aboard the *Intrepid,* one of Admiral Radford's carriers.

"The air groups of Task Group 58.1 and Task Group 58.3

approached the target abeam of each other about 6,000 feet —
the ceiling. The Japanese fleet was sighted at four miles with
only part of the enemy taskgroup visible through broken
clouds at 2,500 feet. Task Group 58.3 planes were directed to
orbit clear of the target. After investigating the enemy formation and finding it in a circular disposition with the *Yamato* at
the center, the planes of Task Group 58.1 were directed to
attack. At the completion of their attack the *Agano* [type
cruiser] was practically dead in the water, listing to port and
burning astern of the formation with one DD to protect her.
The planes of Task Group 58.3 were directed to attack, all VT
[torpedo bombers] and VB [dive-bombers] on the *Yamato* and
the VF [fighters] on the DDS, except the Bataan VT were
ordered to attack the *Agano* and VF the escorting DD."

In other words, it was a well coordinated, patient attack.
The Japanese were below; there were hundreds of American
planes to attack them, and the only thing to be feared was the
Japanese antiaircraft fire. As early in the war off Singapore
and at Pearl Harbor it had been learned that airplanes could
indeed sink battleships, the lesson was told again sharply this
day against the mightiest ship in the world.

Here is a bit of the account from the report of the bombers
of Air Group 83:

"Planes were loaded with 1,000-pound general-purpose
bombs. Fighters initiated the attack, preceding bombers and
torpedo planes; Lt. (j.g.) Gibbs scoring the first hit on the Jap
battleship *Yamato* forward of the superstructure on the port
side. Lt. (j.g.) Scheiss hit a cruiser amidships; Ens. Comstock
10 feet off the bow of one of the destroyers; and Ens. G.
Harris 10 feet off the starboard beam of another destroyer. . . ."

They parceled the targets out. *Yamato* and the other ships
twisted and turned and fought back as gamely as they knew
how. Squadron 83 left her smoking slightly and still under
way. The torpedo planes all went in on *Yamato* and began to
get hits.

Here is part of Torpedo 83's report:

"Lieut. Beeson's division approached from the *Yamato*'s
port bow and entered into the torpedo run just a short interval

f time and distance behind . . . . As the *Yamato* swung to the arboard, its port beam was presented in full and all four ilots declared afterwards that it gave them the best target they ver had at any time in their torpedo training exercise. Lieut. eeson, Lt. (j.g.) Roe and Ens. Shranger all claim hits; pilots nd crewmen among them saw at least two torpedo explo-ions. Ens. Baas was out of position and he observed his tor-edo wake pass astern, run under a *Terutsaki* [destroyer] off ie BB's starboard quarter, and then disappear."

Ensign Barrett, another pilot, also missed *Yamato*, but it as his luck that his torpedo ran hot and straight into the port de of a destroyer on the *Yamato*'s starboard quarter, ex-loded—and the Japanese destroyer sank.

That is the way it went. It seemed that the Americans could o nothing wrong that day, and the Japanese nothing right. If iey had been sent out to show how brave men could accept aughter and overwhelming odds, they did just that. At the id of it, with the hundreds of planes having struck, the .mericans lost just ten planes and twelve airmen.

The Japanese force died in agony. Five torpedo hits in the ort side of *Yamato* made a death trap of the engine and boiler ooms; they had to be flooded, and the flooding caught the ngine room crews, who had no chance.

All in all there were five waves of attack, and each one did iore damage than the last, until by 1620, having fought the ght of her life without hope since just after 1230, the *Yamato* iffered several internal explosions and went down. Three ours later, assessing the damage, Admiral Mitscher reported ▸ Admiral Spruance that they had sunk *Yamato*, a cruiser, a ght cruiser, two destroyers, and had damaged three or four thers that got away. Four destroyers went home, limping, ith some survivors. But *Yamato* lost 2,400 of her 2,700 of-cers and men that day. The cruiser *Yahagi* lost nearly 500, ie cruiser *Asashimo* lost over 300, and on the seven de-royers some 400 men were killed.

After Okinawa was secured, Admiral Spruance departed id soon the Third Fleet was on the rampage, doing what dmiral Halsey loved best and what he did best, hitting the iemy hard where it hurt most. This time, in the summer

months of 1945, the place to hit hard and hurt most was th
Japanese homeland, and it was here that the last bitter end
the Japanese surface navy was played out.

On July 24, the Third Fleet was off the coast of Japan, an
the pilots of the task force were smashing Japanese installa
tions, with so little opposition that it was hardly believable
Of course there was reason. Japanese aircraft factories wei
still functioning, Japan was still fighting the war, but she wa
saving everything for those last desperate hours on th
beaches, when her leaders expected the blood of the invade
to turn the water red.

"Continued to steam in Task Group 38.4 toward the ope
ating area," said the laconic report of *Yorktown* for July 2
"Sweeps and strikes began at 0445 against our prime targe
which was combatant shipping in the vicinity of Kure nav
base." *Yorktown* finished 120 combat sorties, and althoug
damage was difficult to assess *Yorktown* pilots "poured it on" th
AG [transport] *Settsu*, the cruiser *Oyodo*, the light cruis
Hosho, and the cruiser *Tone*, and scored additional heavy dan
age to a minimum of about 14,000 tons of shipping, as well as
six airfields. There was virtually no airbone opposition, exce
over Bungo Suido where ten to twelve Franks and Jacks we
encountered. *Yorktown* pilots shooting down one Jack and dan
aging one. On the airfields, four unidentified aircraft we
destroyed on the ground and nine unidentified were damaged.
addition, three locomotives were destroyed and two damage
plus other attrition to miscellaneous installations.

On the 25th the Third Fleet struck again, and on the 26
and 27th replenished, and on the 28th played out the last
the drama of the naval forces of Japan.

On that 28th again the pilots hit the Kure area.

According to Halsey's records, "An assessment of th
damage for the day revealed that *Yorktown* claimed a numb
of hits and near misses on the *Haruna*, the *Oyodo*, the *Ton*
an old cruiser, and a destroyer or destroyer escort. Phot
graphs showed the main deck of the *Haruna* complete
blown off for a distance of about 65 feet astern of the No.
turret, while the *Oyodo* was last seen by pilots listing heavi
to starboard in an extensive oil slick."

Admiral Halsey's Third Fleet did as much damage in the two air raids on Kure naval base as if they had engaged in a dangerous naval battle at sea. Nine major capital ships were sunk or put out of action. There it was, the end of the Japanese fleet, and the end of the carrier war. Just a few days later came Hiroshima, and the end of it all.